DEPRESSION

THE ENCYCLOPEDIA OF
HEALTH

PSYCHOLOGICAL DISORDERS
AND THEIR TREATMENT

Solomon H. Snyder, M.D. · General Editor

DEPRESSION

Dianne Hales

Introduction by C. Everett Koop, M.D., Sc.D.
Surgeon General, U.S. Public Health Service

CHELSEA HOUSE PUBLISHERS
New York · Philadelphia

The goal of the ENCYCLOPEDIA OF HEALTH *is to provide general information in the ever-changing areas of physiology, psychology, and related medical issues. The titles in this series are not intended to take the place of the professional advice of a physician or other health-care professional.*

Chelsea House Publishers
EDITOR-IN-CHIEF Nancy Toff
EXECUTIVE EDITOR Remmel T. Nunn
MANAGING EDITOR Karyn Gullen Browne
COPY CHIEF Juliann Barbato
PICTURE EDITOR Adrian G. Allen
ART DIRECTOR Maria Epes
MANUFACTURING MANAGER Gerald Levine

The Encyclopedia of Health
SENIOR EDITOR Sam Tanenhaus

Staff for DEPRESSION
ASSOCIATE EDITOR Paula Edelson
COPY EDITOR Karen Hammonds
DEPUTY COPY CHIEF Ellen Scordato
EDITORIAL ASSISTANT Jennifer Trachtenberg
PICTURE RESEARCHER Villette Harris
ASSISTANT ART DIRECTOR Loraine Machlin
SENIOR DESIGNER Marjorie Zaum
PRODUCTION COORDINATOR Joseph Romano

First Printing

1   3   5   7   9   8   6   4   2

Library of Congress Cataloging-in-Publication Data

Hales, Dianne R., 1950–
    DEPRESSION / Dianne Hales ; introduction by C. Everett Koop.
    p.   cm.—(The Encyclopedia of health. Psychological
disorders and their treatment)
    Bibliography: p.
    Includes index.
    Summary: Explores some causes of depression, ways to overcome this
illness, and where and when to seek help.
    ISBN 0-7910-0046-X.—ISBN 0-7910-0512-7 (pbk.)
    1. Depression, Mental—Juvenile literature.   [1. Depression,
Mental.]   I. Title.   II. Series.   88-34176
RC537.H29 1989   CIP
616.85'27—dc19   AC

CONTENTS

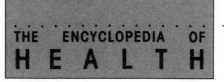

THE ENCYCLOPEDIA OF HEALTH

THE HEALTHY BODY

The Circulatory System
Dental Health
The Digestive System
The Endocrine System
Exercise
Genetics & Heredity
The Human Body: An Overview
Hygiene
The Immune System
Memory & Learning
The Musculoskeletal System
The Neurological System
Nutrition
The Reproductive System
The Respiratory System
The Senses
Speech & Hearing
Sports Medicine
Vision
Vitamins & Minerals

THE LIFE CYCLE

Adolescence
Adulthood
Aging
Childhood
Death & Dying
The Family
Friendship & Love
Pregnancy & Birth

MEDICAL ISSUES

Careers in Health Care
Environmental Health
Folk Medicine
Health Care Delivery
Holistic Medicine
Medical Ethics
Medical Fakes & Frauds
Medical Technology
Medicine & the Law
Occupational Health
Public Health

PSYCHOLOGICAL DISORDERS AND THEIR TREATMENT

Anxiety & Phobias
Child Abuse
Compulsive Behavior
Delinquency & Criminal Behavior
Depression
Diagnosing & Treating Mental Illness
Eating Habits & Disorders
Learning Disabilities
Mental Retardation
Personality Disorders
Schizophrenia
Stress Management
Suicide

MEDICAL DISORDERS AND THEIR TREATMENT

AIDS
Allergies
Alzheimer's Disease
Arthritis
Birth Defects
Cancer
The Common Cold
Diabetes
First Aid & Emergency Medicine
Gynecological Disorders
Headaches
The Hospital
Kidney Disorders
Medical Diagnosis
The Mind-Body Connection
Mononucleosis and Other Infectious Diseases
Nuclear Medicine
Organ Transplants
Pain
Physical Handicaps
Poisons & Toxins
Prescription & OTC Drugs
Sexually Transmitted Diseases
Skin Disorders
Stroke & Heart Disease
Substance Abuse
Tropical Medicine

PREVENTION AND EDUCATION: THE KEYS TO GOOD HEALTH

C. Everett Koop, M.D., Sc.D.
Surgeon General,
U.S. Public Health Service

The issue of health education has received particular attention in recent years because of the presence of AIDS in the news. But our response to this particular tragedy points up a number of broader issues that doctors, public health officials, educators, and the public face. In particular, it points up the necessity for sound health education for citizens of all ages.

Over the past 25 years this country has been able to bring about dramatic declines in the death rates for heart disease, stroke, accidents, and, for people under the age of 45, cancer. Today, Americans generally eat better and take better care of themselves than ever before. Thus, with the help of modern science and technology, they have a better chance of surviving serious—even catastrophic—illnesses. That's the good news.

But, like every phonograph record, there's a flip side, and one with special significance for young adults. According to a report issued in 1979 by Dr. Julius Richmond, my predecessor as Surgeon General, Americans aged 15 to 24 had a higher death rate in 1979 than they did 20 years earlier. The causes: violent death and injury, alcohol and drug abuse, unwanted pregnancies, and sexually transmitted diseases. Adolescents are particularly vulnerable, because they are beginning to explore their own sexuality and perhaps to experiment with drugs. The need for educating young people is critical, and the price of neglect is high.

Yet even for the population as a whole, our health is still far from what it could be. Why? A 1974 Canadian government report attributed all death and disease to four broad elements: inadequacies in the health-care system, behavioral factors or unhealthy life-styles, environmental hazards, and human biological factors.

To be sure, there are diseases that are still beyond the control of even our advanced medical knowledge and techniques. And despite yearnings that are as old as the human race itself, there is no "fountain of youth" to ward off aging and death. Still, there is a solution to many of the problems that undermine sound health. In a word, that solution is prevention. Prevention, which includes health promotion and education, saves lives, improves the quality of life, and, in the long run, saves money.

In the United States, organized public health activities and preventive medicine have a long history. Important milestones include the improvement of sanitary procedures and the development of pasteurized milk in the late 19th century, and the introduction in the mid-20th century of effective vaccines against polio, measles, German measles, mumps, and other once-rampant diseases. Internationally, organized public health efforts began on a wide-scale basis with the International Sanitary Conference of 1851, to which 12 nations sent representatives. The World Health Organization, founded in 1948, continues these efforts under the aegis of the United Nations, with particular emphasis on combatting communicable diseases and the training of health-care workers.

But despite these accomplishments, much remains to be done in the field of prevention. For too long, we have had a medical care system that is science- and technology-based, focused, essentially, on illness and mortality. It is now patently obvious that both the social and the economic costs of such a system are becoming insupportable.

Implementing prevention—and its corollaries, health education and promotion—is the job of several groups of people:

First, the medical and scientific professions need to continue basic scientific research, and here we are making considerable progress. But increased concern with prevention will also have a decided impact on how primary-care doctors practice medicine. With a shift to health-based rather than morbidity-based medicine, the role of the "new physician" will include a healthy dose of patient education.

Second, practitioners of the social and behavioral sciences—psychologists, economists, city planners—along with lawyers, business leaders, and government officials—must solve the practical and ethical dilemmas confronting us: poverty, crime, civil rights, literacy, education, employment, housing, sanitation, environmental protection, health care delivery systems, and so forth. All of these issues affect public health.

Third is the public at large. We'll consider that very important group in a moment.

Fourth, and the linchpin in this effort, is the public health profession—doctors, epidemiologists, teachers—who must harness the professional expertise of the first two groups and the common sense and cooperation of the third, the public. They must define the problems statistically and qualitatively and then help us set priorities for finding the solutions.

To a very large extent, improving those statistics is the responsibility of every individual. So let's consider more specifically what the role of the individual should be and why health education is so important to that role. First, and most obviously, individuals can protect themselves from illness and injury and thus minimize their need for professional medical care. They can eat a nutritious diet, get adequate exercise, avoid tobacco, alcohol, and drugs, and take prudent steps to avoid accidents. The proverbial "apple a day keeps the doctor away" is not so far from the truth, after all.

Second, individuals should actively participate in their own medical care. They should schedule regular medical and dental checkups. Should they develop an illness or injury, they should know when to treat themselves and when to seek professional help. To gain the maximum benefit from any medical treatment that they do require, individuals must become partners in that treatment. For instance, they should understand the effects and side effects of medications. I counsel young physicians that there is no such thing as too much information when talking with patients. But the corollary is the patient must know enough about the nuts and bolts of the healing process to understand what the doctor is telling him. That is at least partially the patient's responsibility.

Education is equally necessary for us to understand the ethical and public policy issues in health care today. Sometimes individuals will encounter these issues in making decisions about their own treatment or that of family members. Other citizens may encounter them as jurors in medical malpractice cases. But we all become involved, indirectly, when we elect our public officials, from school board members to the president. Should surrogate parenting be legal? To what extent is drug testing desirable, legal, or necessary? Should there be public funding for family planning, hospitals, various types of medical research, and medical care for the indigent? How should we allocate scant technological resources, such as kidney dialysis and organ transplants? What is the proper role of government in protecting the rights of patients?

What are the broad goals of public health in the United States today? In 1980, the Public Health Service issued a report aptly entitled *Promoting Health-Preventing Disease: Objectives for the Nation.*This report expressed its goals in terms of mortality and in terms of intermediate goals in education and health improvement. It identified 15 major concerns: controlling high blood pressure; improving family planning; improving pregnancy care and infant health; increasing the rate of immunization; controlling sexually transmitted diseases; controlling the presence of toxic agents and radiation in the environment; improving occupational safety and health; preventing accidents; promoting water fluoridation and dental health; controlling infectious diseases; decreasing smoking; decreasing alcohol and drug abuse; improving nutrition; promoting physical fitness and exercise; and controlling stress and violent behavior.

For healthy adolescents and young adults (ages 15 to 24), the specific goal was a 20% reduction in deaths, with a special focus on motor vehicle injuries and alcohol and drug abuse. For adults (ages 25 to 64), the aim was 25% fewer deaths, with a concentration on heart attacks, strokes, and cancers.

Smoking is perhaps the best example of how individual behavior can have a direct impact on health. Today cigarette smoking is recognized as the most important single preventable cause of death in our society. It is responsible for more cancers and more cancer deaths than any other known agent; is a prime risk factor for heart and blood vessel disease, chronic bronchitis, and emphysema; and is a frequent cause of complications in pregnancies and of babies born prematurely, underweight, or with potentially fatal respiratory and cardiovascular problems.

Since the release of the Surgeon General's first report on smoking in 1964, the proportion of adult smokers has declined substantially, from 43% in 1965 to 30.5% in 1985. Since 1965, 37 million people have quit smoking. Although there is still much work to be done if we are to become a "smoke-free society," it is heartening to note that public health and public education efforts—such as warnings on cigarette packages and bans on broadcast advertising—have already had significant effects.

In 1835, Alexis de Tocqueville, a French visitor to America, wrote, "In America the passion for physical well-being is general." Today, as then, health and fitness are front-page items. But with the greater scientific and technological resources now available to us, we are in a far stronger position to make good health care available to everyone. And with the greater technological threats to us as we approach the 21st century, the need to do so is more urgent than ever before. Comprehensive information about basic biology, preventive medicine, medical and surgical treatments, and related ethical and public policy issues can help you arm yourself with the knowledge you need to be healthy throughout your life.

FOREWORD

Solomon H. Snyder, M.D.

Mental disorders represent the number one health problem for the United States and probably for the entire human population. Some studies estimate that approximately one-third of all Americans suffer from some sort of emotional disturbance. Depression of varying severity will affect as many as 20 percent of all of us at one time or another in our lives. Severe anxiety is even more common.

Adolescence is a time of particular susceptibility to emotional problems. Teenagers are undergoing significant changes in their brain as well as their physical structure. The hormones that alter the organs of reproduction during puberty also influence the way we think and feel. At a purely psychological level, adolescents must cope with major upheavals in their lives. After years of not noticing the opposite sex, they find themselves romantically attracted but must painfully learn the skills of social interchange both for superficial, flirtatious relationships and for genuine intimacy. Teenagers must develop new ways of relating to their parents. Adolescents strive for independence. Yet, our society is structured in such a way that teenagers must remain dependent on their parents for many more years. During adolescence, young men and women examine their own intellectual bents and begin to plan the type of higher education and vocation they believe they will find most fulfilling.

Because of all these challenges, teenagers are more emotionally volatile than adults. Passages from extreme exuberance to dejection are common. The emotional distress of completely normal adolescence can be so severe that the same disability in an adult would be labeled as major mental illness. Although most teenagers somehow muddle through and emerge unscathed, a number of problems are more frequent among adolescents than among adults. Many psychological aberrations reflect severe disturbances, although these are sometimes not regarded as "psychiatric." Eating disorders, to which young adults are especially vulnerable, are an example. An extremely large number of teenagers diet to great excess even though they are not overweight. Many of them suffer from a specific disturbance referred to as anorexia nervosa, a form of self-starvation that is just as real a disorder as diabetes. The same is true for those who eat compulsively and then sometimes force themselves to vomit. They may be afflicted with bulimia.

Depression is also surprisingly frequent among adolescents, although its symptoms may be less obvious in young people than they are in adults. And, because suicide occurs most frequently in those suffering from depression, we must be on the lookout for subtle hints of despondency in those close to us. This is especially urgent because teenage suicide is a rapidly worsening national problem.

The volumes on Psychological Disorders and Their Treatment in the ENCYCLOPEDIA OF HEALTH cover the major areas of mental illness, from mild to severe. They also emphasize the means available for getting help. *Anxiety and Phobias, Depression,* and *Schizophrenia* deal specifically with these forms of mental disturbance. *Child Abuse* and *Delinquency and Criminal Behavior* explore abnormalities of behavior that may stem from environmental and social influences as much as from biological or psychological illness. *Personality Disorders* and *Compulsive Behavior* explain how people develop disturbances of their overall personality. *Learning Disabilities* investigates disturbances of the mind that may reflect neurological derangements as much as psychological abnormalities. *Mental Retardation* explains the various causes of this many-sided handicap, including the genetic component, complications during pregnancy, and traumas during birth. *Suicide* discusses the epidemiology of this tragic phenomenon and outlines the assistance available to those who are at risk. *Stress Management* locates the sources of stress in contemporary society and considers formal strategies for coping with it. Finally, *Diagnosing and Treating Mental Illness* explains to the reader how professionals sift through various signs and symptoms to define the exact nature of the various mental disorders and fully describes the most effective means of alleviating them.

Fortunately, when it comes to psychological disorders, knowing the facts is a giant step toward solving the problems.

•   •   •   •

AN EPIDEMIC OF SADNESS

Abraham Lincoln was said to have experienced severe depression.

Depression is one of the oldest human afflictions. Hippocrates, the ancient Greek healer, described patients who suffered from "melancholia," a condition with the same symptoms as what we now call major depression, including the inability to feel pleasure, loss of appetite or weight, early morning awakening, lack of energy, and excessive or inappropriate guilt.

DEPRESSION

The ancient Greek physician Hippocrates.

In the 16th century, William Shakespeare described similar symptoms in one of his best-known characters, Hamlet. Sinking into despair, Hamlet laments:

> How weary, stale, flat and unprofitable
> Seem to me all the uses of this world!

Even more profound was the severe depression that Abraham Lincoln suffered when he wrote the following words:

> I am now the most miserable man living. If what I feel were equally distributed to the whole human family, there would not be one cheerful face on earth. Whether I shall ever be better, I cannot tell; I awfully forebode I shall not. To remain as I am is impossible. I must die or be better, it appears to me.

Today, the pain of depression remains just as intense and as widespread. According to the American Psychiatric Association (APA), about one of every five Americans experiences an episode of depression in his or her lifetime. Moreover, the median age for depression, and for its most drastic consequence—suicide—has fallen. Indeed, depression has become a growing problem among children and adolescents. The APA estimates that 3 to 6 million young people may currently be depressed.

Depression involves a vast spectrum of issues. As a serious illness, it can take many forms, including major depression, which engulfs its victims in physical lethargy and profound psychological misery, and manic, or bipolar, depression, in which a sufferer's mood swings from frenzied highs to despairing lows. Some people live in a chronic state of sadness that is called dysthymia.

According to the APA, nearly 80% of all people who fall victim to depression fail to recognize the illness and to get the help they need. Instead, they attribute their weariness and aches to the flu or to "some bug that's going around." If they cannot eat or sleep and lose their ability to enjoy pleasure, they blame "stress." If they cannot concentrate or think clearly, they believe their lack of sleep is the culprit. Unaware of the real problem, they suffer— with no solution in sight.

Depression can appear at any age, even in infancy. According to the APA, more than half the people who experience one episode of major depression will have another at some point in their life. Sometimes many years pass before the ailment recurs; sometimes it recurs within a period of weeks. About 20%–35% of all depressed people are chronically troubled.

Albrecht Durer's 1514 engraving Melancholia. *Almost 80% of depressed people fail to recognize their problem and get the help they need to recover.*

Medical research has provided new insight into the roots of depression. It is now known that genes play a major role, and researchers have identified a genetic marker (a sequence of bases within a gene that serves especially to identify a gene or a trait linked to it) that indicates susceptibility to manic depression. All forms of depression tend to run in families, and children with depressed parents seem particularly vulnerable to depression—and at an earlier age than youngsters with parents who are not depressed. Among the other factors that may contribute to depression are stressful life events such as a job or school change or a divorce and losses such as the death of a loved one.

In addition to understanding more about how and why depression begins, therapists have become more effective in bringing depression to an end. Various forms of "talking therapy," or psychotherapy, have proved helpful for mild to moderate depressions, and antidepressant medications provide relief to those with more serious or biologically based depressions. With treatment, 80%–90% of depressed individuals start feeling better within a few weeks.

But for those who do not seek or receive help, depression can be life threatening. According to the *American Psychiatric Press Review of Psychiatry* (1988), 60% of all people who commit suicide are depressed.

The suicide rate for young adults between the ages of 15 and 24 has tripled in the last 30 years, according to the National Center for Health Statistics. Every day 13 young men and women succeed in killing themselves.

Yet dangerous depression can be overcome. More and more depressed people are learning what may be the most important lesson of their life, that, as one woman who struggled with depression put it, "at the end of even the longest tunnel is light."

• • • •

CHAPTER 1

. . . .

WHAT IS DEPRESSION?

Sooner or later everyone feels blue. Our spirits sag and we slide down in the dumps for a few days. Sometimes our feelings of depression are a symptom of another problem, such as the flu or a hormonal imbalance or a normal and temporary reaction to a traumatic event. Within a week or two, the colors of our dark blue world brighten, and we start feeling better.

Depression strikes people of all racial, ethnic, and economic groups. One out of every 10 people develops some form of the illness at some point in his or her life.

Unlike the feeling of depression, which comes and goes, the disease of depression persists and deepens over several weeks or months. No bad mood feels quite so miserable, lasts so long, or seems so endless. A medical disorder that is as real and as serious as diabetes or pneumonia, depression affects the body as well as the mind, trapping its victims in a bleak cocoon of hopelessness and helplessness.

Depression is a common ailment of modern society. No one is immune. People of all ages and of every social, racial, ethnic, and economic group can become victims. According to the *American Psychiatric Press Textbook of Psychiatry* (1988), at any given time 9%–20% of all people suffer some of the symptoms of depression, and 4%–6% are experiencing a major depression. The *Textbook of Psychiatry* estimates that more than 10% of the population are likely to develop depression at some point in their life.

Although the essential features of depression are similar for adults, adolescents, and children, some differences do emerge among the three age groups. According to the *Diagnostic and Statistical Manual of Mental Disorders (DSM)*, published by the

American Psychiatric Association, symptoms for prepubertal children may include physical and psychological restlessness and hallucinations (usually only a single voice talking to the child), anxiety disorders, and phobias. Adolescents may exhibit negative or aggressive behavior; feel restless, grouchy, and misunderstood; be reluctant to participate in family ventures; withdraw from social activities; have difficulty in school; pay little attention to personal appearance; and use alcohol and/or drugs. Of course adolescence is always a difficult time, and any teenager exhibits any or all of these forms of behavior at some point. But constant and excessive displays of these symptoms may be a sign of serious depression. Symptoms of depression for adults may include sleep disturbances, loss of interest in sex, loss of appetite or weight, lethargy, and physical symptoms such as constant stomach upset.

DEFINING AND DIAGNOSING DEPRESSION

Perhaps the simplest definition of depression is, as Harvard Medical School psychiatrist Ned Gassem said, "misery requiring treatment." Depressed people are not merely unhappy but pro-

Many teenagers have difficulty concentrating in school. But if taken to extremes and accompanied by other symptoms such as social withdrawal and drug use, this behavior may be a sign of depression.

foundly miserable. They lose interest in food, friends, sex, favorite activities, or any form of pleasure. They lack energy but often cannot sleep. Their thoughts are consistently negative, even when good things happen. They believe there is no end to the despair and self-loathing that they constantly feel. Often, they consider suicide.

Medical researchers have developed several laboratory tests that detect various biological changes in blood, urine, or sleep patterns linked to depression. None, however, provides definitive proof that a person is or is not depressed.

The DSM bases its diagnosis of clinical depression on the presence of at least five of the following symptoms nearly every day for two weeks:

- Depressed mood. Depressed people may be tearful, irritable, or anxious. They often feel that they do not care anymore—about themselves, their loved ones, or anything that once brought them joy.

- Loss of interest in activities. Depressed people do not enjoy what are usually thought of as pleasurable activities—sports, socializing with friends, and even eating do not seem to bring them any pleasure.

- Significant weight loss or gain or decreased or increased appetite. Because they are rarely hungry, some depressed people lose a considerable amount of weight. Others, particularly young women, overeat or go on eating binges and gain weight.

- Insomnia or hypersomnia (excessive sleep). Some depressed people either have trouble falling asleep or awake constantly during the night. Others spend more time than usual sleeping and have a great deal of difficulty getting out of bed in the morning.

- Psychomotor agitation or retardation. Some victims of depression cannot stay still and are constantly wringing their hands or pacing. Others move and talk much less often and much more slowly than usual.

- Fatigue or loss of energy. Inertia, or inability to become motivated, immobilizes many depressed people; even the smallest tasks seem to be too demanding for them to handle.

- Feelings of worthlessness or inappropriate guilt. Some depressed people become convinced that they utterly lack worth and view even the most trivial failure as proof of their inadequacy. If they do badly on a pop quiz, for instance, they are convinced that they are a failure.

- Diminished ability to think or concentrate. Depressed individuals cannot focus their thoughts and often seem indecisive. The thoughts that they do have are usually unpleasant. If a friend does not return a phone call, they immediately conclude that nobody likes them.

- Thoughts of suicide or death. Depressed people often feel that if they died, they or their loved ones would be better off. They may brood about the end of their own life and plan or attempt suicide.

Police treat a man who jumped from the 96th floor of the Empire State Building and landed on a ledge 5 floors below. Depression that is not properly treated can destroy lives; 15% of those diagnosed as being depressed eventually commit suicide.

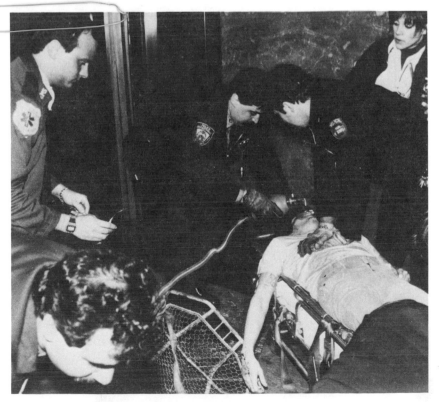

Depression varies in severity. People who are mildly depressed have minimal symptoms that cause only minor problems in their academic, professional, or social life. Moderate depression involves more symptoms and a greater impact on day-to-day functioning. Persons who are severely depressed experience numerous symptoms that markedly interfere with their ability to work, study, and get along with others.

If it seems as though some or all of these symptoms apply directly to you, take heart; at times we all feel depressed. You may lose your appetite, toss and turn at night, pull away from your family and friends. But before you seek professional help, compare what you are feeling with the intensity of the symptoms associated with clinical depression. It could be that your symptoms are not only minor but completely normal.

A TREATABLE PROBLEM

"Depression is probably the most widespread, most extensively studied and best understood major psychiatric disorder," notes psychiatrist Martin Keller, M.D., of Harvard Medical School. Yet, according to the APA, less than 33% of depressed people seek treatment.

Many victims of depression do not realize they are ill and may not seek help. Some may think seeing a therapist is a sign of weakness, so they suffer alone. But, if left untreated, depression can last for months and recur throughout a person's lifetime, shattering careers and relationships and undermining physical well-being. This life-threatening problem can claim as well as cripple lives. According to the DSM, about 15% of those diagnosed as depressed commit suicide.

But depression, like many other illnesses, can be overcome. With help, most depressed individuals begin feeling better within weeks and can soon rebuild their battered sense of self-esteem and regain their belief in themselves and their hope in a brighter future.

●   ●   ●   ●

CHAPTER 2

· · · · · · · · · · · · · ·

HISTORY OF DEPRESSION: AN OVERVIEW

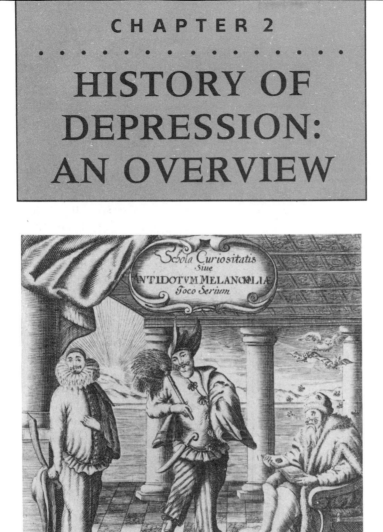

A 17th-century German engraving shows actors cheering up a melancholy scholar.

Depression has been a part of human existence since ancient times. As scientists have discovered more about the human body and psyche, theories of the cause and treatment of the disorder have changed. Speculations about the ailment have progressed from the ancients' discussion of "humors" to 20th-century breakthroughs that have traced some types of depression to chemical imbalances in the brain.

MELANCHOLIA IN ANCIENT TIMES

According to the ancient Greek physician Hippocrates, who lived in the 5th century B.C., the symptoms of melancholia included "an aversion to food, despondency, sleeplessness, irritability, and restlessness." Hippocrates and his followers believed that human health was determined by the relative levels of the four humors: blood, yellow bile, black bile, and phlegm. Each humor was thought to be most prevalent during a particular season; blood in spring, yellow bile in summer, black bile in autumn, and phlegm in winter. Each humor was associated with a combination of descriptions: blood with warm and moist, yellow bile with warm and dry, black bile with cold and dry, and phlegm with cold and moist.

To these ancient scientists, specific diseases stemmed from specific imbalances in the humors. Depression, for instance, indicated trouble with black bile. In *Melancholia and Depression: From Hippocratic Times to Modern Times*, Stanley Jackson, professor of psychiatry at Yale University, states that "scattered references" in Hippocrates' writings suggest that "melancholia was one condition among several termed melancholic diseases, that the black bile was the key factor in causing such diseases, that autumn was the season when a person was at particular risk from the effects of this humor, that the black bile was viscous in nature and associated with the qualities of coldness and dryness, and that such a syndrome with its mental disturbances was surely the result of the brain being affected."

A century after Hippocrates wrote, the Greek philosopher Aristotle (384–322 B.C.) also associated melancholia with an imbalance of humors. He believed, however, that black bile was not cold and dry, as Hippocrates argued, but rather a combination of heat and cold. If a patient's black bile grew too cold, he or she would then suffer melancholia. Another ancient thinker, the Roman encyclopedist Celsus (circa A.D. 30), who was influenced by both Hippocrates and Aristotle, asserted that "the black bile disease supervenes upon prolonged despondency with prolonged fear and sleeplessness." He also recommended various treatments, including bloodletting (draining of blood), massage, exercise, and "entertainment sought by storytelling and by games, especially by those with which the patient was wont to be attracted when sane; work of his, if there is any, should be praised,

Depicted here teaching Alexander the Great, the Greek philosopher Aristotle (right) believed that melancholia stemmed from specific imbalances in the four humors.

and set out before his eyes; his depression should be gently reproved as being without a cause; he should have it pointed out to him now and again how in the very things which trouble him there may be cause of rejoicing than of solicitude."

The Roman anatomist and physician Rufus of Ephesus, who lived during the age of Trajan (A.D. 98–117), drew up a list of symptoms of melancholia and stressed that the chief indications of the ailment were fear and doubting, though other signs, such as anxiety and delusions, might also appear. Rufus believed the disorder struck men more often than women. He also broke it down into three general types: One type affects only the brain; a second affects the whole body; a third affects only the upper abdomen. These classifications lasted for several centuries.

The Greek physician Galen (A.D. 129–circa 199) accepted Rufus's theory and concurred with the theories of the humors proposed by Hippocrates and Aristotle. He added that the spleen was the organ capable of clearing black bile out of the blood unless there was an excess of this humor, which would then

Galen, a Greek physician who lived and practiced in ancient Rome, thought that the spleen cleared black bile out of the body. If there was an excess of this humor, it congealed in the stomach and caused melancholia.

congeal in the stomach and "prevail all over the body," causing melancholia. Galen's contemporary Aretaeus (2nd century A.D.) also broke with tradition by proposing for the first time that melancholia and mania, a condition characterized by intense euphoria and delusions of grandeur, might be related diseases and, moreover, that the two conditions were symptoms of a single disorder.

THE MIDDLE AGES

Ancient theories of melancholia, especially those formulated in the writings of Galen, persisted among medieval physicians. One such, Alexander of Tralles (circa 525–605), who practiced in Rome, listed as symptoms of melancholia fear, rage, and euphoria and suggested that suicidal and homicidal tendencies might both result from this disorder. He also offered, according to *Melancholia and Depression*, three causes of melancholia: an excess of blood, a stoppage of blood, and an excess of black bile. Alexander recommended that people afflicted with depression should bathe, cleansing themselves of their melancholia, and speak with close friends.

Another medieval scientist who studied melancholia was the Islamic physician Ishaq ibn Imran, who lived in the early 10th century. He was strongly influenced by the writings of Galen and Rufus and held that people were either born with a disposition to melancholia or could acquire it through "neglect of the internal cleanliness of the body" and through "too much rest and sleep."

THE RENAISSANCE

Ancient hypotheses continued to dominate thinking on melancholia during the Renaissance, which peaked in the 15th century. In fact, most scientists of this era agreed with the theories of Hippocrates and Galen. There were some original thinkers, however. One was the German physician Paracelsus (1493–1541), who rejected the humoral theory of behavior and proposed his own theory on temperaments. Paracelsus identified four temperaments, or complexions—bitterness, saltiness, sourness, and sweetness—and linked melancholia with a sour temperament. Paracelsus's ideas would eventually become influential in the 17th and 18th centuries.

In 1621, British clergyman and author Robert Burton (1557–1640) published a survey of Renaissance ideas about melancholia called *The Anatomy of Melancholy*. This remarkable book—a masterpiece of world literature—indicates that most Renaissance scientists and physicians bowed to the ancient view that melancholia was caused by an excess of black bile. Burton's text also points out that the scientists of his day accepted Rufus's classification of three different types of melancholia. *The Anatomy of Melancholy* urges patients to employ a treatment that combines prayer, medication, diet, and the solace of talking with friends. Burton concludes his treatise by advising all victims of melancholia to "be not solitary, be not idle."

THE SEVENTEENTH CENTURY

In the second half of the 17th century, concepts of melancholia began to evolve. The humoral theory gave way to more scientific explanations. One reason new ideas emerged was that melancholia had become a fashionable ailment, a mark of distinction and intelligence; it can even be said that the disorder had a certain amount of mystique attached to it. The result was that an increasing number of people admitted to being stricken with melancholia, thus providing researchers with more opportunities to study its causes and consequences.

Richard Napier (1559–1634), a British physician and clergyman, initially accepted the humoral theory, but as his knowledge of it grew during the early years of his practice, Napier came to believe the disease actually sprang from several different causes. According to *Melancholia and Depression*, Napier "held the view that astrological factors had predisposed a patient to suffer a mental disorder peculiar to his particular temperament, but such factors were not sufficient to explain his illness. . . . Although a variety of supernatural causes, either divine or diabolical, were commonly held responsible for mental disturbances in Napier's time, he seldom attributed such disorders to God; but he accepted the view that Satan might well be responsible in some cases." Napier also argued that if someone suffered a trauma, such as an illness or a stressful event, a melancholic episode might ensue.

Insights into melancholia also came from the British anatomist and physician Thomas Willis (1621–75). In *Two Discourses Concerning the Soul of Brutes* (published in 1672), Willis categorized melancholia into two divisions: universal, in which sufferers are "delirious as to all things, or at least as to most; so that they judge truly almost of no subject"; and particular, in which victims "imagine amiss in one or two particular cases." Willis dismissed the humoral theory and said that the true cause of melancholia was the combination of brain and heart maladies.

Although Willis and Napier both rejected the humoral theory as a possible cause of melancholia, neither discovered revolutionary treatments for the disorder. Both recommended gentle medications and the solace of friends. Nevertheless, these two physicians were instrumental in advancing theories on melancholia—ideas that would be more dramatically altered during the next centuries.

THE EIGHTEENTH CENTURY

Many 18th-century theories on the cause of melancholia lay in what were called "mechanical" explanations. This philosophy held that human physiology partly depended on the motion and interaction of various particles. Those who believed and studied mechanical theory included the English scientist Isaac Newton, discoverer of gravity.

One of the first researchers to apply mechanical explanations to melancholia was the British anatomist Archibald Pitcairn (1652–1713). In *The Philosophical and Mathematical Elements of Physick* (1718), Pitcairn defines disease as "an unusual Circulation of Blood, or the circular Motion of the Blood augmented or diminished, either throughout the whole Body, or in some Part of the Body." He then claims that melancholia, which he describes as a delirium without fever, arose as a result of a "Defect" of "vivid Motions."

Pitcairn's contemporary Friedrich Hoffmann (1660–1742) also supported the mechanical theory. Hoffmann stressed that melancholia arose as a defect in the circulation of the major body fluids, which he believed were the blood, lymph spirits, and animal spirits. When these spirits flowed indirectly and thus grew acidic, Hoffmann wrote, motions became sluggish, and the per-

Eighteenth-century theorist Richard Mead hypothesized that a person's mood depended on the amount of "nerve fluid" in the brain.

son turned irritable, moody, and sad. Like several scientists before him, Hoffmann believed mania and melancholy were aspects of a single illness.

Another significant 18th-century theorist was Richard Mead (1673–1754), a student of Pitcairn and a friend of Isaac Newton's. Mead added to Hoffmann's and Pitcairn's ideas by introducing the notion of "nerve juices." According to *Melancholia and Depression*, Mead, who also believed that melancholy and mania were interrelated, "conceived of excitement and collapse as states of increased and decreased mobility of the nervous power or nervous fluid in the brain."

As popular as the mechanical theory of melancholia proved in its time, it soon gave way to new theories. One critic of the theory, William Cullen (1710–90), claimed melancholy and mania were caused not by changes in circulation of body fluids but by increased or decreased levels of the brain's "nervous power."

Even as theories came and went, treatments remained the same. Doctors prescribed an easily digestible diet, exercise, gentle hypnotics, and again, cheerful conversations with friends.

THE NINETEENTH CENTURY

Studies of melancholia in the 19th century begin with the American physician Benjamin Rush (1745–1813). In *Medical Inquiries and Observations upon the Diseases of the Mind* (1812), Rush set

American physician Benjamin Rush, depicted here, believed that melancholia was a form of madness that originated in the circulatory system.

An 1804 cartoon of bloodletting. This practice, which originated in ancient Greece, was a popular treatment for melancholia until the 20th century.

forth the theory that depression was a form of madness and that all such diseases originated in the vascular (or circulatory) system. "The cause of madness is seated primarily in the blood-vessels of the brain, and . . . it depends upon the same kind of morbid and irregular actions that constitutes other arterial diseases." Rush prescribed that melancholic patients try bloodletting—a remedy employed since medieval times—bathing, exercise, and a reduced diet that would soothe the action of the blood vessels.

The French physician Jean-Étienne-Dominique Esquirol (1772–1840) wrote extensively on melancholy. He believed the disorder had numerous causes and was also related to other forms of insanity. He listed among its symptoms a fear without object or cause—what we today call "anxiety." The causes he gave included hereditary factors, which he deemed were most important, and then psychological elements, such as family problems, financial worries, and childbirth.

Several years after Esquirol published his ideas, the German scientist Wilhelm Griesinger (1817–68) presented his theories about melancholia. The disorder, Griesinger maintained, has three distinct and separate causes: psychic, mixed, and physical. The psychic causes, the most common, can be attributed to grief, loss of fortune, injury, illness, or even a spoiled love affair. The mixed causes of depression, said Griesinger, include drunkenness and sexual deprivation; physical causes include nervous disorders, head injuries, disorders of various organs, pregnancy, and childbirth.

Griesinger emphasized that treatment of melancholia should begin early and that different patients require different remedies. In cases where the causes are psychic, he favored removing the patient from his or her surroundings for rest and quiet. In the other two instances, he advised a regulated diet, abstinence from alcohol, and an abundance of exercise.

The British physician and author John Charles Bucknill (1817–97) added to the studies of melancholia with *A Manual of Psychological Medicine* (1858), which he coauthored with D. Hack Tuke (1827–95), another British scientist. Bucknill insisted that melancholia the disease should be distinguished from "normal and healthy grief and sorrow, of which all men have their share in this chequered existence." He also argued that certain people inherit a predisposition to develop the ailment. Bucknill listed the main symptoms of melancholia as "sorrow, despondency, fear, and despair, existing in a degree far beyond the intensity in which these emotions usually affect the sane mind."

One of the most influential of the 19th-century theorists was the German neuropsychiatrist Richard von Krafft-Ebing (1840–1902). He divided mental disorders into two categories: mental diseases and arrested development. He placed melancholia in the first category, under the subcategory "psychoneurosis," and identified two types of the disease. In the first type, the patient suffered delusions; the second, milder form—"simple melancholia"—occurred more often and was more easily treatable.

In *Text-Book on Insanity* (1904), Krafft-Ebing outlined his ideas for treatment: (1) "Give the patient complete physical and mental rest." (2) "Surveillance of the patient to protect him from himself and others from him." (3) "Care of the general condition and of the amount of food taken." (4) "Treatment, by proper means, of sleeplessness, which is very exhausting and favors the development of delusions and hallucinations." (5) "Use of symptomatic remedies approved by experience." For this last treatment, Krafft-Ebing suggested the use of opium, which in the 19th century was commonly prescribed by physicians, who did not yet realize its dangerous and addictive nature.

The 19th-century German neuropsychiatrist Richard von Krafft-Ebing prescribed opium—a drug whose addictive nature was unknown at the time—for the treatment of depression.

THE TWENTIETH CENTURY

In the 20th century, there have been major developments in the theory of melancholy—by this time called depression—and manic depression. A pioneer in the study of the latter was German psychiatrist Emil Kraepelin (1856–1926), who classified a single disease that involved both melancholia and mania as "manic-depressive insanity." He wrote about mania in a sequence of forms ranging from mild to severe: "hypomania," "mania," and "delirious mania."

Kraepelin also classified depressive states. The first he designated "simple retardation," the mildest form of the disorder, wherein the sufferer can see only the dark side of life and perceives unhappiness in past, present, and future. A more severe type of depression is "retardation with delusions and hallucinations," in which the victim may suffer some delusions of persecution and some physical symptoms, such as numbness, constipation, and heart palpitations. Finally, Kraepelin listed "stuperous conditions," which constitute the most severe form of depression. This depression is characterized by numerous dreamlike delusions and hallucinations, which permanently cloud the sufferer's consciousness.

Manic depression, according to Kraepelin, is a disease more common in women than in men, and 70%–80% of its victims inherit a predisposition to the disorder. In fact, Kraepelin noted, the disease itself is a physical one with a neuropathic, or neurological, basis. Kraepelin also remarked that in most cases manic depression can be temporarily treated but very few of its victims recover completely. For that reason, he recommended that victims of all but the mildest disorders should stay in an asylum, where special precautions could be taken against the possibility of suicide.

Kraepelin's contemporary was the American psychiatrist Adolf Meyer (1866–1950). He agreed with some of Kraepelin's theory concerning depression and mania but stressed psychological rather than physical causes. According to *Melancholia and Depression*, Meyer "argued for a careful assessment of the patient's situation and pathological reaction . . . with an eye to determining how the particular person's disturbed condition might have developed and what might be modified or treated." Meyer also thought depression could occur by itself or be accompanied by other psychiatric disorders.

No discourse on the history of any psychological disorder would be complete without the opinions of the Viennese psy-

Adolf Meyer, an American psychiatrist, held that the nature of depression was psychological rather than physical.

Sigmund Freud believed that depression arose when there was a conflict between two of the forces of the human mind—the superego and the ego.

chiatric pioneer Sigmund Freud (1856–1939). Freud pinned much of his theory on the existence of three categories of the human mind: the *id*, which includes reflexes and unconscious desire; the *ego*, or the conscious mind; and the *superego*, which internalizes parental and societal rules. Freud proposed that melancholia occurs when the superego "abuses" the ego—"threatens it with the direst punishment . . . represents the claims of morality, and we realize all at once that our moral sense of guilt is the expression of the tension between the ego and the superego" (*New Introductory Lectures on Psycho-Analysis*, 1933). Freud determined that melancholia was strictly the result of psychological factors—a view many adhered to but others criticized as the century advanced.

CONTEMPORARY THOUGHTS

Modern research on the cause and treatment of depression indicates that depression and manic-depressive illness are complex disorders that involve biological, psychological, and social factors. No specific biological cause or defect has been linked to depression—no bacteria or virus, no abnormal hormone, enzyme, or other body chemical. But there is strong evidence that the disorder is somehow related to changes in chemicals situated in the brain, called neurotransmitters, whose function is to help pass messages from one nerve cell to another. These changes

35

possibly result from some inherited genetic defect, though there may be other reasons as well. The two neurotransmitters most often implicated are serotonin and norepinephrine.

At the same time, there are those who agree with Freud and his colleague Karl Abraham (1877–1925) that the root of depression is psychological. One such psychiatrist, René A. Spitz (1887–1974), determined that infants who were separated from their mothers for long periods of time suffered such symptoms as sadness, withdrawal, antisocial behavior, loss of appetite, and insomnia—all signs of clinical depression.

Treatment for depression differs, of course, according to whether the cause is deemed psychological or biological. Most psychiatrists agree, however, that the most effective remedy is a mixture of drug therapy and psychological therapy. Lithium, an antipsychotic salt, has proved remarkably effective in controlling the mood swings caused by manic depression, and other drugs, such as the antidepressants trazodone, trimipramine, and desipramine, help balance serotonin and norepinephrine levels in the brain.

In sum, theories on the cause and treatment of depression have recently gained in sophistication. Until the 17th century, most theorists thought depression was the result of an excess of black bile. This idea was rejected in favor of other biological possibilities, such as the notion that the disorder was caused by problems in the vascular or neurological systems. The 19th and early 20th centuries saw the beginnings of the theory that depression is a psychological disorder. Today, although scientists still disagree about the cause of the illness, the advent of antidepressant drugs—and the improvement of psychiatric therapy—have made the treatment of depression more successful and humane than ever before.

•   •   •   •

CHAPTER 3

TYPES OF DEPRESSION

Mental health professionals classify depression as a "mood" disorder, that is, a disorder that affects a person's thoughts and feelings. The moods themselves depend on the type of depression the patient is suffering. For example, a person with bipolar, or manic, depression swings wildly from frantic highs to numbing lows, whereas a person with unipolar depression experiences only the lows. Both types of depression, however, cause major-depressive episodes characterized by bleak moods, irritability, sadness, pessimism, anger, anxiety, hostility, guilt, irritability, and a conviction that their misery will never end.

MAJOR DEPRESSION

A major-depressive episode can occur at any age, but it is usually first experienced by people in their late twenties. According to the *American Psychiatric Press Textbook of Psychiatry*, major depression is twice as common in women as in men and 1.5 to 3 times more common among people with close biological relatives who have been similarly afflicted. About 9%–26% of women and 5%–12% of men in the United States develop major depression.

Several factors increase a person's susceptibility to an episode of major depression, including chronic physical illness and dependence on alcohol, cocaine, or other drugs. Some people suffer an episode of major depression after the death of a loved one, marital separation, or divorce. Occasionally childbirth precipitates a major depressive episode in new mothers; this is called postpartum (after birth) depression, and is a type of clinical depression that can range from mild to severe.

Major depression, which sometimes develops over a period of days or weeks and sometimes occurs suddenly, always interferes to some extent with social and occupational functioning. In severe cases, the person may be unable to work, study, and interact with people and may sometimes be incapable of feeding, clothing, or cleaning him- or herself.

Without treatment, a major-depressive episode typically lasts for six months or more. Usually victims recover completely and return to the same level of functioning they had had before the illness struck. However, some symptoms, such as depressed mood and lack of pleasure or appetite, can persist for as long as two years. The most serious complication of major depression is the increased risk of suicide.

Some people suffer a single episode of major depression and then return to normal functioning. But more than half suffer a second episode. Episodes may be separated by many years of normal functioning or they may occur in a cluster. Some people

Postpartem depression, which affects some women shortly after childbirth, is a type of clinical depression that can range from mild to severe.

experience increasingly frequent episodes as they grow older. In 20%–35% of all cases, symptoms and social impairment persist, and depression never completely lifts.

DYSTHYMIA

The simplest definition of dysthymia is prolonged sadness. Dysthymic adults experience deep and lasting depression without significant change in mood for at least two years. In children and adolescents, dysthymia may last for as little as one year.

Usually dysthymic individuals also suffer at least some of the symptoms of depression: poor appetite or overeating, sleeping too little or too much, low energy or fatigue, low self-esteem, problems thinking and concentrating, and feelings of hopelessness. These symptoms may become so severe that, in addition to dysthymia, sufferers develop major depression and experience what therapists call "double depression."

Dysthymia is often linked to other problems, such as anorexia nervosa (an eating disorder characterized by an obsession with thinness and extreme weight loss through dieting or strenuous exercise), drug abuse, and anxiety. According to the *Diagnostic and Statistical Manual*, it strikes equal numbers of male and female children but is "apparently more common" among adult women than men. This statistic could be inaccurate, however, because women are more likely than men to seek help. Close biological relatives of individuals with major depression run a higher risk of developing dysthymia than the general population.

This disorder usually develops in childhood, adolescence, or early adulthood but does not have a precise, clear beginning. Children and teenagers are more likely to become dysthymic if they suffer from hyperactivity, conduct disorders, mental retardation, developmental problems, or if their parents go through a difficult divorce or are alcoholic or abusive.

Dysthymia often affects young people's relationships and interactions with peers and adults. When depressed, they may exhibit unsocial behavior—such as objecting to or withdrawing from praise—possibly as a means of "testing" or of venting resentment and anger. School performance and progress may deteriorate. The treatment for dysthymia is the same as that for depression: psychotherapy, drug therapy, or a combination thereof.

MANIC DEPRESSION

Manic depression, which therapists refer to as bipolar illness, is the most dramatic mood disorder. Its victims moods swing from depression to the opposite extreme—euphoria. About 1 of every 100 people suffers from manic depression at some point. Usually manic depression begins in a person's twenties, and most cases develop before age 35. Men and women are affected in equal numbers. A manic episode is more likely to occur after major life stresses, childbirth, or as the result of some antidepressant treatments such as drugs or electroshock therapy. Because the victim's social and occupational functioning can be severely impaired, he or she may require hospitalization.

The Dutch Postimpressionist artist Vincent van Gogh suffered major depressive episodes, culminating in suicide in 1890.

At the beginning of a manic phase, patients feel suddenly elated or happy; within a few days this feeling begins to impair their thinking, judgment, and behavior. Among the characteristic symptoms of mania are

- An extremely or inappropriately cheerful mood; inflated self-esteem and unwarranted optimism. Believing themselves invincible or specially empowered by God or political leaders, manic individuals may feel they can do anything—even leap off a high building without being hurt. They may give advice on subjects about which they know little or start writing a novel or composing music even if they have no training or talent.

- Excessive activity. Manics may plan or participate in far more activities than they have time for, scheduling several meetings, parties, and other commitments for the same day. In their frenzied state, manics engage in pleasurable activities in potentially hazardous ways: They may drive recklessly, spend money impetuously, and socialize constantly.

(continued on page 44)

Patty Duke: A Case Study

In 1982, the actress Patty Duke discovered that she was a manic-depressive. For many, this diagnosis would seem an ominous foreshadowing of trauma and treatments. For Duke, however, the news came as a hopeful answer to her lifelong struggle with alternating bouts of rage and despondency. Instead of being unable to understand why she could never lead a stable life, Duke could now work to overcome a specific ailment.

Born into an impoverished family in New York, Anna Marie Duke always dreamed of becoming an actress. When she was eight years old, her mother placed her in the care of John and Ethel Ross, a wealthy couple who immediately began to prepare young Anna Marie for the world of theater. Five years later, Duke became famous when she portrayed young Helen Keller on Broadway in *The Miracle Worker*. She went on to star in her own television series, which ran for three years. This success was not the glamorous culmination of an American teenager's existence; rather, her acting career proved to be the only aspect of her life that she could control.

The Rosses' often suffocating command over their charge began almost immediately, when they changed Duke's first name to Patty. What would appear to be a relatively moderate alteration proved extremely dramatic to the young actress, who viewed it as a threat to her identity. In fact, this development damaged Duke as much as any of the psychological abuses the Rosses inflicted: as much as the regular scrutiny and criticism, as much as the constant programming of what to say in public.

It was on the stage, then, under the control of no one but herself and with the accolades of an audience applauding her, that Duke felt happiest. Despite critical acclaim and high earnings, Duke's problems with the Rosses worsened. Both Rosses were alcoholics, and Ethel was addicted to various drugs. The couple involved Duke in their substance abuse, giving her alcoholic drinks and injecting her with various prescription drugs, including the antipsychotic drugs Thorazine and Stelazine. John Ross's abuse was also physical—he attempted to molest Patty twice, but she successfully resisted.

Because she could only compare this cruelty to her seven years with a weak mother and an alcoholic father, Duke was never certain that the Rosses treated her unjustly. But she was psychologically unstable, suffering daily anxiety attacks as well as anorexia, an eating disorder in which a person can literally starve him- or herself to death. Ironically, it was Ethel's own mother who urged Patty to get out of the situation. At 19, Patty Duke, television's ideal of an American teenager but in reality exhausted and traumatized, left the Rosses to marry Harry Falk, her show's assistant director, whom she later divorced. (Duke's second marriage, to actor John Astin, also ended in divorce. In 1986 she married businessman Michael Pierce.)

But although Duke was away from the Rosses, she still experienced extreme emotional confusion and regular outbursts. In her autobiography, *Call Me Anna*, Duke describes the feeling of being out of control, common to many manic-depressives. Without any external provocation, Duke would begin screaming at her husband, inflamed with anger and unable to understand why or stop the incident. Likening the driving force in these rages to "some demonic engine," Duke came to rely on alcohol and Valium for peace; she even attempted suicide a few times when the drug-induced sleep did not relieve her trouble.

Unfortunately, it took Duke a long time to seek professional help. Because she had been mistreated throughout most of her life, Duke tended to blame her problems on her own inability to overcome the prolonged abuse. But finally, Duke found the advice—and the diagnosis—that she needed. Following this breakthrough, Duke stopped trying to stabilize herself with self-assigned tranquilizers. Instead, her doctor prescribed an appropriate medication, lithium, to help neutralize the imbalance of chemicals that causes her disorder.

After her diagnoses, Duke returned to her acting career, and she eventually became president of the Screen Actors Guild. In 1987, Duke published her autobiography, which served both as a final catharsis from her many years of struggle and as a source of hope to others who suffer manic-depression.

(continued from page 41)

- Racing thoughts. Manic individuals think so fast that loosely associated ideas pour out of their mouth. Their speech is loud, rapid, and filled with puns and word plays. They leap from topic to topic so quickly that others may not be able to interpret their ramblings.

- High energy. Manic patients may go for days with little or no sleep without feeling tired. When they do go to bed, they often wake up hours before dawn, full of energy. They also often have difficulty concentrating and may shift attention in the middle of a sentence to unimportant details or unrelated topics.

- Irritability or anger. If their grandiose plans are not realized, manics may become enraged or paranoid (highly suspicious of others).

A hypomanic episode is one in which a person's mood is extremely elevated, but the disturbance is not so severe that it impairs social and occupational functioning or requires hospitalization. If untreated, a manic or hypomanic phase can last as long as three months. Some patients return temporarily to normal mood and behavior; others immediately plunge into an episode of major depression. Scientists have found that there may be a genetic predisposition to manic depression, and that the disease itself is caused by a chemical imbalance in the brain.

Manic or hypomanic stages almost always alternate with periods of depression, which resemble major or unipolar depression. The symptoms are decreased energy, fatigue, inability to experience pleasure, loss of interest in life, inability to concentrate, withdrawal, insomnia or excessive sleep, appetite and weight changes, physical complaints, feelings of worthlessness and guilt, and thoughts of death or suicide.

Bipolar illness often begins with a depression in adolescence or early adulthood; the first manic episode may not occur for several years. Manic attacks tend to come and go very quickly, whereas depressions are slower to develop and to disappear. Most victims of manic depression are level between their periods of disordered mood. Some are never free of lingering symptoms.

CYCLOMANIA

As its name may imply, people with cyclomania experience alternating episodes of hypomania and depressed mood over a two-year period (one year for children and adolescents). Although the symptoms are similar to those of manic and major depression, the impairment is never extreme.

Some people are highly productive and sociable when hypomanic, whereas others experience difficulties in their relationships, schoolwork, and careers. Cyclomania usually strikes adolescents or young adults. Although the disorder itself is not considered severe, if left untreated it can lead to major- and manic-depressive episodes.

SEASONAL AFFECTIVE DISORDER

Seasonal affective disorder (SAD) is an annual rhythm of depression that appears to be linked to seasonal variations in light. Although the gloomy, gray days of winter can bring anyone down,

Victims of seasonal affective disorder are subject to serious, sometimes debilitating depression during the autumn and winter months.

some people feel more than slightly depressed at this time of year. The reason may be that they are abnormally sensitive to changes in light. This disorder is caused by an overabundance of melatonin, a sleep-inducing hormone that the brain produces only at night. Melatonin may depress mood and thought processes in the winter months. Seasonal variations may contribute to hypomania in the spring.

Although winter depression is far more common than spring depression, researchers at the National Institute of Mental Health in Rockville, Maryland, have identified a reverse form of SAD in which depression develops in the summer and hypomania in the winter. They have not yet developed estimates of how many people may be affected in this manner.

PSYCHOTIC DEPRESSION

About 10% of people suffering from clinical depression experience delusions or hallucinations so severe that they lose touch with reality; this syndrome is called psychotic depression. Hallucinations psychotic depressives perceive may revolve around the feelings commonly associated with depression (guilt, inadequacy, preoccupation with death) or they may involve completely different themes, such as persecution or delusions of control. The disorder can strike any age group; the average sufferer may be in his or her late twenties, but children, teenagers, and older adults are also susceptible. The risk of suicide is five to six times greater for victims of psychotic depression as it is for people who do not suffer any form of depression.

•   •   •   •

CHAPTER 4

· · · · · · · · · · · · ·

WHAT CAUSES DEPRESSION?

Stress is a leading cause of depression.

No one has ever identified a single, dominant cause of depression. Almost always a combination of factors is responsible: genetic vulnerability, a developmental trauma, intense life stresses, physical illness, and environmental and social influences. In some people, biological predisposition may be especially strong. In others, a life crisis may play a greater role.

FAMILY HISTORY

Two-thirds of depressed patients have family members who have suffered depression. Although mild depression does not seem to be inherited, more serious forms run in families. According to the *Diagnostic and Statistical Manual of Depressive Disorders*, immediate biological relatives of a depressed person have a 15% chance of developing depression. Grandchildren, nephews, and nieces have a 7% risk. A person with no relatives who have suffered depression has about a 2%–3% risk of developing the disorder.

A study of 200 young people ranging in age from 2 to 23 by the epidemiologist Myrna Weissman of Columbia University, reported in the *American Psychiatric Press Review of Psychiatry* (1988), suggests that those with depressed parents are at an especially high risk of developing major depression, anxiety disorders, and other psychiatric disturbances. They also show signs of major depression much earlier in life than children of parents who are not depressed.

GENETICS

Researchers have identified genetic markers for manic depression on different chromosomes (the rodlike structures within each cell that contain genetic instructions). But they have not found the specific gene or genes for any depressive disorder.

Studies of identical twins—who have the same genes—support the claim that there is a genetic component to depression. If one identical twin develops depression, there is a 70% chance that the other will follow suit. Adoption studies also underscore the significance of genetics. A child of a depressed parent who is adopted at birth into a family with no history of depression is three times more likely to become depressed than is a biological child of the adoptive family.

EARLY LIFE EXPERIENCES

Developmental traumas of childhood, particularly the death of a parent at an early age, can increase susceptibility to depression. Neglect, abuse, and separation from a parent because of illness or divorce can trigger childhood depression and increase the risk of depression in adulthood.

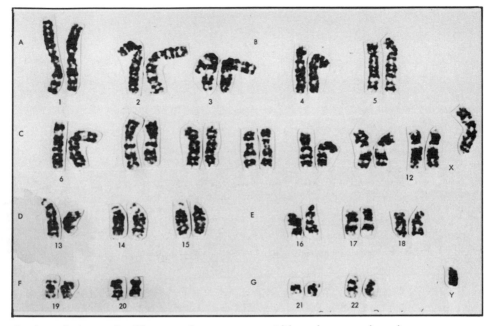

A microphotograph of human chromosomes. Although researchers have found genetic markers for manic depression on certain chromosomes, they have not found a specific gene for any depressive disorder.

PROBLEMS IN RELATIONSHIPS

Attachments dramatically affect our emotional well-being. In general, people involved in stable, close relationships are less likely to be depressed. In adult women, the single most common trigger for major depression is an unhappy love relationship. People who describe their marriages as being in trouble are 25 times more likely to be depressed than those in happy marriages.

Are these individuals depressed because their basic need to love and be loved is blocked? Or does the depression come first, triggering marital problems as the afflicted person withdraws into his or her own misery? According to psychiatrist Steven Dubovsky of the University of Colorado, author of *Clinical Psychiatry* (1988), depressed partners may become irritable, dependent, and sensitive to rejection, "alienating others before they have a chance to leave on their own."

LOSS

The most traumatic losses are those that deprive us of people whom we love: When our parents, grandparents, and friends die, we lose them forever. But if they move, separate, divorce, or

Studies show that if one identical twin suffers depression, the other has a 70% chance of developing the disorder.

remarry, we still may feel depressed. The loss of a game, competition, or prized possession can also be painful. Sometimes the loss is not quite so tangible—the dream of going to college, perhaps, or of getting a job—but the sadness is just as real.

PSYCHOLOGICAL FACTORS

Often people struggling with difficult problems stumble into certain psychological traps, which can increase the risk of depression. Among the most common are

- Unresolved grief. Not mourning or coming to terms with a loss—of a person, a position, even a quality, such as youth or attractiveness—can breed feelings of sadness and anger. With time, these emotions can fester into a deep-rooted sense of unhappiness, low self-esteem, hopelessness, and extreme sensitivity to rejection.

- Suppressed anger. Individuals who feel unable to express the normal anger that develops in daily living—often because they fear rejection—may turn that anger on themselves. This allows them to acknowledge their rage and at the same time to punish themselves for their "unacceptable" feelings.

- Learned helplessness. Sometimes an unavoidable setback, such as an accident or illness, makes a person feel helpless. The condition may then spread to other situations until he or she feels utterly overwhelmed. A disappointment at school or work can have the same effect. A teenager may fail a test, try halfheartedly to study harder for the next one, and fail again. At that point, failure begins to seem inevitable, and the student gives up.

PHYSICAL ILLNESS

Depression can also occur as a complication of a physical disease. Any serious disease can cause depression, but some actually cause physical problems that can result in clinical depression. Hypothyroidism, for example, is a deficiency of thyroid hor-

Disappointments, such as failing a test, often cause depression in teenagers.

mones, which may change the body's and brain's chemical balance. In a report published in *Seminars in Adolescent Medicine* in December 1986, child psychiatrists Linda Gourash and Joaquim Puig-Antich of Western Psychiatric Institute and the University of Pittsburgh noted that 8%–14% of all depressed patients have low thyroid hormone levels and recommend testing the thyroid function of all depressed teens. The tiny pathogens that cause viral infections, such as hepatitis and mononucleosis, can sap physical strength and, in unknown ways, undermine psychological well-being.

Premenstrual syndrome (PMS) is another physical syndrome with psychological side effects. According to Gourash and Puig-Antich, a "large proportion" of women who seek treatment for PMS have symptoms of depression, and two-thirds of women who have a major-depressive episode report premenstrual aggravation of their depressive symptoms.

Medications taken for various medical problems can be culprits, as well. Depression has been linked to the use of birth control pills, steroids, and drugs that control high blood pressure.

Left: *One neuron signals another by emitting a neurotransmitter such as norepinephrine across a synapse.* Right: *Each neurotransmitter fits one kind of receptor on the target neuron.*

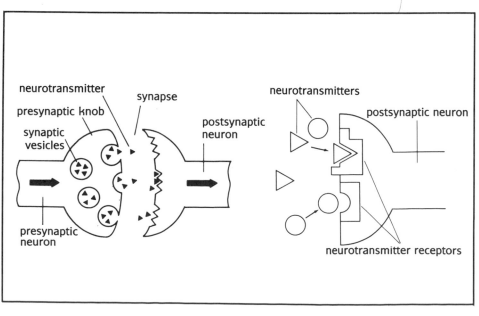

Depression often strikes people who feel trapped by circumstances. Single mothers who must work to support their children, for example, are prime candidates for this disorder.

Excessive caffeine—in coffee or stimulants—may also contribute to depression. Some over-the-counter diet pills have been linked to depressive episodes in teenagers.

CHANGES IN BRAIN CHEMISTRY

Depression alters the delicate balance of certain chemicals, including two crucial brain chemicals—serotonin and norepinephrine—that enable brain cells to communicate with each other. An imbalance of serotonin may be responsible for the sleep problems, irritability, and anxiety suffered by many depressed people. Irregularities in norepinephrine, which regulates alertness and arousal, may contribute to fatigue and depressed moods.

Among the other body chemicals that become imbalanced in cases of depression is cortisol, the major hormone produced by the adrenal gland. The secretion of cortisol is regulated by the pituitary gland, which in turn is regulated by the hypothalmic region of the brain. The abnormal patterns of cortisol secretion may derive from imbalances of serotonin and norepinephrine in the brain.

53

ENVIRONMENTAL FACTORS

Environmental stress plays an important role in depression. People who feel trapped or overwhelmed by circumstances—such as single working mothers with young children—are prime targets for depression.

Even happy events, such as graduation or going away to college, increase the likelihood of depression. Often expectations soar so high that reality can never equal the anticipation. And although many milestones mark new beginnings, they also spell the end of valued periods in our life. Graduation, for instance, may be the door to the adult world, but it is also the time for leaving close friends and taking on new responsibilities.

DRUG AND ALCOHOL ABUSE

Alcoholics and drug abusers suffer high rates of depression, and depressed individuals have a high incidence of substance abuse. The double whammy of these linked disorders takes a devastating toll on physical and psychological well-being.

Which comes first: depression or drug use? No one knows for sure. Many people, particularly teens, may drink or try drugs in the effort to lift their spirits. Researchers have found that depressed young people are especially likely to "self-medicate" and try to boost their moods by using marijuana.

UNDERSTANDING WHY

Often, particularly with a therapist's help, patients can identify several factors that may have triggered their depression. But sometimes the ailment strikes for no apparent reason. Just like dozens of other diseases, depression can happen suddenly and without warning. There is no more reason to blame its victims for their misery than there would be to blame individuals with appendicitis for their illness.

•   •   •   •

CHAPTER 5

. . . .

DEPRESSION IN YOUNG PEOPLE

For many years, mental health professionals thought depression was an "adults-only" disorder, one that did not occur during the carefree days of childhood and adolescence. But in truth, depression can invade at any age and rob any life of joy and hope. An infant who is not touched or held may exhibit depressive symptoms, and many researchers believe this condition may even interupt normal physical development. A depressed toddler might not speak or play, and teen suicides have become so common that some experts believe they have reached epidemic proportions. Fortunately, there are ways to treat childhood or adolescent depression. In fact, the prospects for recovery are in some ways brighter for the young than for adults.

DEPRESSION IN CHILDREN

Why should a baby feel blue? No one knows precisely. Any child with depressed parents is five times more likely to become depressed, but scientists do not know if the reason is genetic or related to the way the parents interact with the child. Probably it is both: Children can inherit a predisposition to depression, and their environment may place them at even greater risk.

In a study of 24 babies and their mothers, published in the professional journal *Child Development* in 1983, psychologists Jeffrey Cohn and Edward Tronick of the University of Massachusetts found that 3-month-old infants definitely noticed—and disliked—the difference in their mothers when they looked and acted depressed. They either protested by crying, fussing, writhing, or arching their backs or became wary, wearing serious expressions and narrowing their eyes. The babies' distress persisted even when the mothers behaved normally again. Infants of mothers suffering serious depression show clearly abnormal behavior, including prolonged rage.

Preschoolers can also become depressed. In a 1987 study of of 109 youngsters between the ages of 2 and 7 (published in the *American Journal of Psychiatry*), 9 children were found to have symptoms of depression. These children did not necessarily seem sad, however. Their depression took the form of anger, restlessness, worry, pains in their arms, legs, and stomach, fears, self-blame, irritability, apathy, tension, or fatigue.

According to child psychiatrist Donald McKnew, Jr., of the National Institute of Mental Health, between 6% and 10% of children ages 6 to 12 have experienced at least 1 episode of major depression. Although they rarely announce, "I'm depressed," they do sometimes complain about being bored and whine or fidget a lot. Often these youngsters have low self-esteem, poor social skills, and tend to withdraw or to become aggressive and angry.

Massive changes, especially those involving loss, as in a divorce or move, may trigger childhood depression. Often children seem

Preschool youngsters are not immune to depression. Symptoms for these children include anger, irritability, and fatigue.

to recover from a loss quickly, but appearances may be deceptive. After losing a special pet, a close relative, or a good friend, a child may relive the pain again and again—even before adulthood—before finally coming to terms with it. Family members may not connect a depression with an event that happened months before, but for the child, that event may be just as real as when it happened.

Pain and illness can cause depression in children as well as in adults. Frustration and failure, sometimes caused by learning disabilities, can lead to depression by damaging the person's self-esteem. Children who sense that they are not living up to their parents' expectations may feel unloved and unlovable.

Therapists diagnose depression in children by observing and interviewing them. When asked direct questions, such as "Are you sad? Do you cry a lot? Have you ever thought of hurting yourself?" even very young children give honest, direct answers.

Child psychologists and psychiatrists specialize in the emotional problems of youngsters. In therapy, they often ask children to make drawings of themselves, their families, and their friends. Using the sketches as starting points, the therapists raise issues that may be troubling a child, such as divorce or a move to a

Massive change, such as the loss of a pet or close friend, is a primary cause of childhood depression.

new town. They observe and talk with children as they play in order to ferret out signs of an underlying problem. Some sessions may include the parents, who can learn to recognize and address a child's fears and provide reassurances of their love. Often children improve dramatically within a few months. "Kids are at a more flexible, fluid state," notes McKnew. "With psychotherapy you can often help, console, advise children in ways that cannot possibly touch adults."

If children fail to improve, antidepressant drugs often help. However, these medications have not been thoroughly tested in children, so psychiatrists cannot gauge the potential long-term effects.

THE UPS AND DOWNS OF ADOLESCENCE

Almost by definition, adolescence is a time of turmoil. All teenagers experience wide mood swings, one day soaring with enthusiasm, the next wanting to huddle under the bedcovers and banish the world. Their bodies change in dramatic, often unsettling, ways. A girl may think she is too tall or fat; a boy may worry about developing his beard or the alarming surges in his

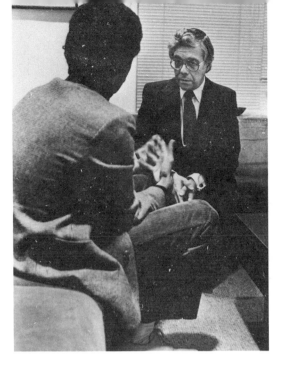

Therapists diagnose depression in teenagers and young adults by observing them and interviewing them.

sexual desire. All may be sure that no one could look as strange, act as weird, or feel as miserable as they do.

Teens' sense of self—and of self-esteem—is so shaky that a cruel word or cold look can shatter it. "I don't care," they will say indifferently, all the while caring with every fiber of their being. Peer acceptance is not merely important; it is often vital. Teens excluded from a clique may conclude that they will never be accepted by anyone in their life.

In addition to feeling scrutinized by their friends and classmates, teenagers think they are constantly being watched and judged by everyone, especially their peers. They see themselves as actors and actresses, performing before an invisible audience that notices everything: the smallest pimple, the slightest clumsiness, the most insignificant slipup.

Adolescents also face an enormous challenge: figuring out who they are and what they want to become. As they question or reject parental beliefs and values, teenagers must sort out their own needs, desires, and goals. The psychiatrist Erik Erikson, who formed important theories of psychological and social development, argued that a crucial crisis for teenagers is attaining a sense of identity while overcoming identity confusion. In *Life History and the Historical Moment* (1975), he describes adolescence as a time of uncertainty, a time when deep down you are not quite sure that you are a man . . . or a woman . . . that you will ever grow again and be attractive, that you will be able to master your drives, that you really know who you are, that you know who you want to be, that you know what you look like to others, and that you will know how to make the right decisions without once and for all committing yourself to the wrong friend, sexual partner, leader or career.

WHY ARE SO MANY SO SAD?

Given the bouts of self-doubt and misery that are part of adolescence, it is not surprising that some teenagers become depressed. What is surprising—and baffling—is just how common depression is and how often it is mistaken for something else.

Psychiatrist Javad Kashani and his colleagues at the University of Missouri-Columbia surveyed 150 local adolescents between the ages of 14 and 16. According to their report, published in the *American Journal of Psychiatry* in July 1987, 8% of the adolescents studied exhibited symptoms of a serious depressive disorder. Girls with these symptoms outnumbered boys five to one. The study also showed that all the depressed youngsters had other problems, including anxiety, drug abuse, and conduct disorders.

Often the same factors that cause depression at other life stages contribute to adolescent depression:

Loss The loss may be an obvious one, such as the divorce of parents, a grandparent's death, breaking up with a boyfriend or girlfriend, or moving to a new city or school. Sometimes losses that may not seem major to an adult are traumatic for a teenager because of the deeply felt attachments that are developed during one's formative years. A series of losses, however small, may make a teen feel that life has lost all meaning.

Low Self-esteem A teenager who gets a poor grade may say, "I should have tried harder." If mildly depressed, he or she might think, "I'm dumb." As depression grows, he or she may say, "I hate myself for being so worthless." Self-criticism can become so extreme that depressed teens feel responsible for everything wrong in the world, and feel they should be punished. Tragically, many decide to punish themselves.

Loneliness Adolescents, particularly between the ages of 12 and 16, report more loneliness than other age groups. The reasons may be that they are separating from their parents, losing their childhood identity, becoming more aware of their own separateness, and that they are forging their first serious relationships.

Stress Adults do not have a monopoly on pressures and tensions, but the stresses that teens encounter are somewhat different. In one study conducted at Vanderbilt University in 1985, researchers asked a group of adolescents complaining of stomachaches, headaches, and chest pain about recent stressful events (good and bad) in their life and about the impact the events had had on them. Topping the list of the 20 most frequently named stressors were failing grades, followed by increasing arguments between (not with) parents, serious family illness, and breaking up with a boyfriend or girlfriend.

Alcoholism and Drug Abuse According to the National Institute on Alcohol Abuse and Alcoholism, almost half of high school seniors get drunk at least once every two weeks. As many as 1.3 million teens are problem drinkers. Teenagers may turn to drugs to lift their spirits, only to feel even worse once they sober up or come down after a high.

More than 1 million teenagers in the United States are problem drinkers.

Poor Coping Skills Teenagers can master the intricacies of computer data bases and of irregular French verbs, but solving life problems is another matter. If they see adults handling stress by drinking, taking drugs, or threatening to leave or to commit a destructive act, they may think the only solutions for problems are negative ones.

RECOVERY

In spite of the hopelessness teenagers feel while they are in the throes of depression, treatment can help them feel better about themselves and the future. Like many adolescents, Tracy, a 15 year old who had become depressed after her parents separated, felt no one could help her. When her mother insisted she see a therapist, she agreed because she was too exhausted to argue.

In her sessions with the therapist, Tracy began to put into words her feelings and fears about her parents' breakup. Many of her sentences began, "If only I . . ." As the therapist pointed out, she was blaming herself—wrongly—for the separation. As they talked, Tracy revealed that as the third of three daughters she had always felt unwanted. Tracy's parents sat in on some of the sessions. With the therapist's help, they were able to reassure Tracy that she was not the reason for their separation and that they did indeed want, love, and care for her.

As Tracy learned to express her emotions, including the scary ones, such as anger and fear, the gray fog of her depression began to lift. She still felt saddened by her parents' decision to get a divorce, but she was able to stop blaming herself, to acknowledge her strengths as well as her weaknesses, and to believe once again that she deserved to be happy.

It should not be forgotten that most depressed teenagers do not require psychological therapy. In fact, therapy is usually prescribed only in severe cases of depression that last for six months or more. The large majority of cases of adolescent depression disappear by themselves.

•   •   •   •

CHAPTER 6

· · · · · · · · · · · · · ·

NO TOMORROW: SUICIDE

No conscious action is more final or more absolute than suicide. It leaves no time for regrets or second thoughts. It is, quite simply, the end.

According to the *American Psychiatric Press Review of Psychiatry* (1988), some 29,000 Americans take their own life each year, and as many as 10 times that number may attempt suicide. The National Center for Health Statistics reports that between

1955 and 1980 the suicide rate among women aged 15 to 20 doubled, and the rate among young men of the same age more than tripled. The rates have not risen since 1980—nor have they dropped. The *Review of Psychiatry* (1988) notes that suicide has become the second (to automobile accidents) leading cause of death for 15 to 24 year olds. Every 1¾ hours a young American— someone with "everything to live for"—commits suicide. Why? It is the question every parent, every relative, every friend asks. "Didn't they know we loved them?" they wonder. "Didn't they know we cared?" The answer is no. Suicide victims feel horribly alone, unloved, and unlovable. Death seems the best, if not the only solution—for their families and friends as well as themselves.

More teenage girls than boys attempt suicide, often taking drug overdoses or slashing their wrists. But more teenage boys actually kill themselves, in part because they choose more lethal means, such as guns.

MYTHS ABOUT SUICIDE

Because suicide is a difficult subject for people to think or talk about, many misconceptions about it persist. Among the most common are

- People who talk about killing themselves never do. Actually, most people who commit suicide do give clear verbal and/or behavioral warnings and should be taken seriously. Their words are pleas for help.

- Talking about suicide in front of a depressed person might give him or her suicidal ideas. In truth, bringing up the subject may actually help depressed people talk about their feelings.

- If someone wants to commit suicide, no one can do anything to prevent it. Untrue. Most people who kill themselves want to live but do not see any other way out.

- Any person who becomes suicidal will always be that way. In fact, the despair and helplessness that lead to suicide are temporary. With help, suicidal persons can lead a full, happy, productive life.

Emergency workers rescue a young woman who is trying to jump off a building. More than half of all teens who attempt suicide are depressed.

- If someone improves after a suicide attempt, there is no reason for further concern. This is a dangerous misconception. If the person gets no help, the second try may seem even easier. Eighty percent of suicide victims attempted suicide at least once before. A repeated attempt often occurs about three months after what seems like a period of improvement.
- People who try to kill themselves are crazy. Actually, suicidal people are extremely unhappy but not necessarily mentally ill. Most are depressed; few are psychotic.

UNDERSTANDING TEEN SUICIDE

No theory can explain a phenomenon as complex as the surge in adolescent suicides. More than half of all the teens who attempt suicide are depressed. But teenagers who have never shown any signs of depression can and do kill themself.

Some may act impulsively in a fit of rage or frustration. Often teenagers attempt suicide while under the influence of alcohol or drugs. Some experts speculate that many have a sense of immortality and do not believe death is final; others feel that circumstances, particularly a long string of pressures and losses, may culminate in a sense of entrapment so overwhelming that teens see no alternative except to take their own life.

Often teens who attempt suicide are locked in conflict with their parents over poor grades, skipping school, delinquent behavior, or drug use. The final straw may be a disciplinary crisis, a fight with a boyfriend or girlfriend, or any incident that intensifies a youngster's feelings of despair, humiliation, rejection, fear, and inadequacy. Sometimes teenagers see suicide as an act of revenge, a way of getting back at those who have hurt them in the past.

RISK FACTORS FOR SUICIDE

Two teenagers may have parallel life experiences, encountering similar traumas and disappointments. Both may become discouraged and distraught. Suicide might never occur to one; the other may see it as a logical solution. Why are some individuals more susceptible to suicidal thoughts and actions? The answers are not clear, but psychologists and other therapists have identified various factors that may contribute to the risk of adolescent suicide, including the following.

Biological and Genetic Factors Adults who attempt suicide have abnormal levels of serotonin, a messenger chemical in the brain. In order to understand how serotonin and other chemical neurotransmitters work, it is essential to examine the workings of the neuron. This is a cell specialized for the transmission of information. Information is carried between neurons by means of neurotransmitters, or chemical messengers, an exchange that takes place at junctions between neurons, known as synapses. At a synapse, the axon, or extension, of a neuron makes contact with the dendrites, or branches, of another. The end of the axon, when properly stimulated, releases neurotransmitters into the region between the two neurons. These molecules then reach specific receptors located on the second neuron, which then becomes stimulated in its own right.

Serotonin is a neurotransmitter thought to be involved in sleep and also in sensory perceptions; according to psychiatrist Herman van Praag of the Albert Einstein College of Medicine in New York City, a low level of serotonin seems to be a biochemical marker for those depressed people who are most prone to suicide. Genetics may also contribute to susceptibility; suicide does appear to run in families.

Parents' Psychological Problems Chronic emotional illness in parents—including depression, substance abuse, and suicide attempts—increases the risk of suicide for children. In a study published in the *Journal of the American Academy of Child Psychiatry* in 1984, epidemiologist Myrna Weissman of Columbia University compared 194 youngsters, all between 6 and 18 years of age, of depressed and more stable parents. Of those with depressed parents, 6.5% reported suicidal thoughts, and .9% attempted suicide. Children whose parents were not depressed reported no suicidal thoughts or attempts.

Developmental Traumas People who feel deprived, rejected, or unloved during childhood may become angry and resentful when they reach their teens. These emotions are often followed by feelings of guilt and by self-destructive behavior. A history of child abuse has also been linked to subsequent suicide attempts in adolescence.

Precipitating Events Often the stage is set for a suicide attempt by a combination of long-standing problems and a recent emotional crisis, such as pregnancy, change in residence, romantic breakup, injury or illness in self or loved one, separation/ divorce of family members, death of loved one, severe disappointment, or school problems.

Aggressive, Impulsive Behavior Patterns Psychiatric "autopsies" of teens who have killed themselves have revealed that many had displayed rapid mood changes and outbursts of violence and aggression and had a history of problems in school. A close encounter with suicide or attempted suicide—through a parent, sibling, or close friend—may push impulsive, aggressive youths toward suicide.

Failure to Live up to Expectations Parents and teachers can put pressures on teenagers, but sometimes the highest, most unattainable expectations come from within. Teens who constantly strive for perfection may feel they must live up to impossibly high standards, and after even a minor failure or setback, they see no option other than killing themselves. They feel disgraced in the world's eyes—and their own.

Availability of Guns Access to a gun may make it easier for a depressed youth to carry out a self-destructive impulse. According to a 1986 study (published in the *American Journal of Public Health*), suicide rates involving firearms increased 3 times more quickly from 1933 to 1982 than did suicides by other methods for those aged 15 to 19—and 10 times more quickly for those aged 20 to 24.

Alcohol and Drug Abuse Because alcohol and drugs distort thinking and enhance impulsivity, they may contribute to deaths that might not have occurred if the teens had not been drunk or high.

Suicide rates involving guns and other firearms have increased dramatically among teenagers.

Imitation Teen suicides tend to increase after news stories and television movies about suicide. Suicide "clusters" and death pacts have also cropped up from time to time. The teens most susceptible to such behavior often suffer from depression, use drugs or drink heavily, and may have dropped out of school.
They may conclude that attempting suicide is a glamorous way of getting attention or of getting back at their parents or a former boyfriend or girfriend.

Family Disruptions The lack of a stable family life because of drug or alcohol abuse or marital problems may make a teenager feel there is no place to turn. Even teens living in stable homes may consider suicide if they cannot communicate with parents about their unhappiness, loneliness, isolation, or frustration.

Size of Peer Group The huge generation of "baby boomers" who entered adolescence and young adulthood from 1955 to 1980 may be under intense stress because of increased competition. According to a 1988 article on suicidal behavior among adolescents in the *American Psychiatric Press Review of Psychiatry*, suicide rates in 15 to 24 year olds historically have risen and fallen with the percentage of people of this age in the population.

WARNING SIGNALS OF SUICIDE

Most teenagers considering suicide say or do something that should serve as a warning signal. The most obvious is a failed suicide attempt. If nothing changes after an attempt; if they do not get the help they need; or if parents and friends assume there is no continuing problem, teenagers often try again—and, this time, succeed.

People planning suicide may give "hints" with statements such as "It's no use" or "Nothing matters anymore." Often they give away favorite possessions, clean their rooms, or do other things to put their affairs in order. If they had been depressed, they may suddenly and inexplicably become cheerful or calm.

Seeing signs of suicidal behavior in a friend is a frightening experience. Often the most you can hope to do is buy time for a professionally trained adult to intervene and help your friend. That, in itself, is an enormous feat.

Warning signs of suicide include

- Dramatic changes, for no apparent reason, in familiar routines for eating, drinking and sexual activity.
- Increased moodiness.
- Specific suicide threats.
- School essays, poems, or drawings revealing a preoccupation with death.
- Failure or poor performance at school.
- Increased drug and alcohol use.
- Breaking off friendships.
- Failed love relationship.
- Withdrawal from normal activities.
- Extreme sadness and depression.
- Feelings of worthlessness or discouragement.
- Persistent boredom.
- Violent or rebellious behavior.
- Running away from home.
- Drug and alcohol abuse.
- Unusual neglect of personal appearance.
- Difficulty concentrating.
- Radical personality change.
- Frequent complaints about physical symptoms, such as headache or fatigue over a long period of time.
- Delusions or hallucinations.
- Overwhelming sense of guilt or shame.
- Changes in social behavior: inability to sit still, emotional outbursts, crying or laughter.

IF SOMEONE YOU KNOW
TALKS ABOUT SUICIDE . . .

A 17-year-old girl did not believe her former boyfriend when he said he would shoot himself if they did not make up. A 15-year-old boy was afraid to tell the terrible "secret" his best friend had told him: that he was thinking about killing himself. A 12-year-old girl did not want to get in trouble for snooping after reading her sister's diary and discovering she was planning to commit suicide.

In these three cases, the teens who talked or wrote about suicide did kill themselves. Too late, their friends and siblings learned a terrible lesson: It is safest to tell a responsible adult when someone you know talks about suicide—even if that means betraying a confidence or breaking a promise. If you do not tell an adult—a family member, a school counselor, a teacher or a coach—they cannot help.

The publications of the American Psychiatric Association and the National Institute of Mental Health suggest the following strategies:

If you suspect that a friend may be depressed or considering suicide, encourage him or her to talk. If you say, "You're crazy," or "You're going to snap out of this," your friend may withdraw, hiding bleak thoughts from those who could help. Do not challenge or dare your friend. Telling a person considering suicide to go ahead will not shock him or her into rational thinking. It might even push him or her over the edge.

If your friend's plans frighten or sadden you, say so. Show you care. Suggest alternatives or solutions to problems. If you are not making any headway, suggest that both you and your friend talk to an expert.

If your friend admits to having considered suicide, ask gentle questions, such as how or why. If he or she has a definite plan, ask for specifics: If the person plans to take pills, ask what kind or whether he or she has bought them yet. Find out if your friend has access to a gun, or to potentially lethal drugs. You should give this information to your friend's parents or to another responsible adult.

Be highly suspicious if a friend makes a point of saying good-bye or giving you some treasured possession. Ask what he or she is planning. Try to start a conversation about his or her feelings. Be supportive. Assure your friend that suicidal impulses are temporary and that all problems, however big, can be solved.

Follow your instincts. If you suspect your friend may act soon, stay with him or her. Call a suicide hot line. If you must leave, make your friend promise not to take any action until you return or get someone else to take your place. Make sure the environment is safe. Remove weapons, pills, razors, or other dangerous objects.

Even if you feel you have talked your friend out of suicide, let someone in a position of authority know what is going on. A calm or elevated mood does not mean the danger is past. In fact, it could indicate that your friend has resigned him- or herself to dying.

It is scary to hear someone close to you talk about suicide. There are steps you can take, but you cannot "fix" the situation. You *can* get help from counselors trained to deal with suicidal individuals.

Almost every community has a 911 or emergency number you can call. Many cities have suicide hot lines. You can also try a local hospital or community mental health center.

What Family Members Can Do

Suicidal or depressed teens need to know that someone cares and wants to try to understand. They feel they are so worthless and contemptible that no one can or should be concerned about

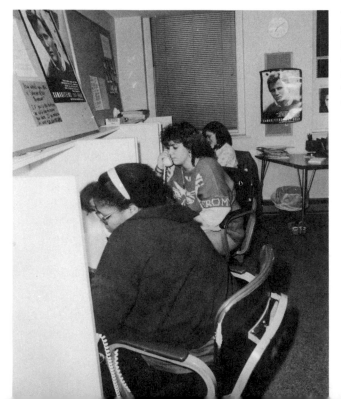

Teenagers answer questions at a suicide prevention center. Such hot lines are available in many cities to console and assist people who are considering suicide.

A CASE HISTORY

"I just didn't know how to keep on living."

All his life, Scott had been—as his parents constantly told him—"the best son anyone could ask for." Then, when Scott was 16, his beloved dog, which he had had for 11 years, was hit by a car. A few weeks later his best friend moved to another state. At a basketball play-off, he missed the foul shot that could have won the game. That same week he failed a chemistry quiz and had a huge argument with his girlfriend.

Convinced he had disappointed everyone he cared about and that no one could possibly care about him, Scott came up with a plan: He would hook up a hose to the exhaust pipe on his mother's car, slide it into a car window, lock the garage doors, and quietly slip away. His plan almost succeeded. But his younger brother came home early, heard the car engine, and broke down the garage door. Paramedics who rushed to the scene were able to resuscitate Scott on the spot.

At the hospital, when Scott saw the anguish on his parents' faces, he felt almost too embarrassed to speak. "We're just glad you're alive," his mother said. "And we love you. We'll always love you. And we're going to help you."

Scott began regular counseling sessions with a therapist who helped him express his feelings of sorrow and failure. He also joined a group of teenagers who had psychological troubles. In the individual and group sessions, Scott talked through his feelings and came to see that, as bad as his problems seemed, they could be dealt with. "I don't think I ever really wanted to die," Scott said six months after his suicide attempt. "I just didn't know how to keep on living."

their welfare. Parents and siblings can provide assurance that teenagers are loved. Listening is crucial. Often parents hasten to warn or comment or criticize. Yet only by being quiet long enough for teenagers to talk can parents find out if their children are distressed. Parents must be especially careful to avoid judgments. Teens who are told "What a stupid thing to say" or "That's dumb" may believe they are indeed stupid. To keep the lines of communication open, parents must be extremely careful not to erect such barriers.

Parents should make sure they support their children not only when they succeed but also when they fail. In that way, teens can learn that they are not the only ones who have ever felt inadequate or incompetent—and that having failed once does not condemn a person to a lifetime of failure.

Often just admitting that their child might commit suicide is hardest for parents. Once they acknowledge that grim possibility, they can focus on preventing its occurrence.

THE SURVIVOR'S BURDEN

Suicide is the ultimate act of rejection, ending one life and shattering many others. Death's sting—always painful—can be excruciating to those left behind: parents, siblings, friends, classmates, colleagues, neighbors. As they mourn for their loved one, they may be haunted by regrets and questions and "if onlys." Survivors are often angry with themselves for not somehow saving the victim. Guilt, which usually subsides after a natural death as mourners come to accept their loss, may linger in the aftermath of a suicide. Survivors may blame themselves for not recognizing clues to the victim's plans. Although the pain of the loss will be with them always, the day usually comes when they can face the future and go on with their life. But one thing never changes. As a mother whose 14-year-old son hanged himself put it, "There's an empty place in your heart forever."

•   •   •   •

CHAPTER 7

OVERCOMING DEPRESSION

The sooner a person realizes that he or she is depressed, the easier it is to break out of the downward spiral. A number of self-help strategies can aid the mildly depressed. More serious and persistent forms of depression, however, require professional treatment.

Studies show that regular exercise is not only a good way to stay physically fit but is healthy for mind and mood as well.

WHAT TO DO WHEN YOU ARE DOWN

As soon as you begin to feel sad and discouraged or as soon as friends or family point out that you have not been your usual self, you can try some strategies to prevent a deepening of depression. These tactics include the following.

Exercise Because depression feeds on inactivity, regular physical workouts can help your mind as well as your body. According to psychiatrist John H. Griest, M.D., a professor of psychiatry at the University of Wisconsin and the author of *Depression and Its Treatment* (American Psychiatric Press, 1986), regular aerobic exercise, such as walking or jogging, significantly improves the mood of mildly depressed college students. Psychiatrist Elizabeth Doyne of the University of Rochester conducted studies that showed that non-aerobic exercises, such as weightlifting, can also help beat the blues.

A self-help center in California. Many hospitals and community health centers sponsor such groups, which can provide help and consolation for sufferers of depression.

Enjoyment Participating in pleasant activities—concerts, excursions, family outings—can also boost your spirits.

Understanding Problems Analyze recent events to identify possible sources of stress. If your life has been particularly tumultuous, arrange a breather. Even a lazy Saturday all to yourself or a weekend away can provide a fresh perspective.

Give Yourself a Break All of us silently "talk" to ourselves every day, commenting on our appearance and behavior. Are you constantly thinking that you look funny or your conversation sounds silly, or do you feel stupid? If so, start editing what you say to yourself. Notice when you are being unrealistically negative or critical and try to focus on things you like about yourself.

A teacher shows her students relaxation techniques. Learning how to identify and handle stressful situations is a good way to minimize depression.

Self-help Groups A sympathetic listener can be enormously helpful as you try to sort out your feelings and thoughts. Individuals who have struggled with depression often find that talking with people who have had similar problems is useful. Many hospitals and community mental health centers sponsor such self-help groups.

TREATING DEPRESSION

Any person whose normal functioning has been inhibited by depression for more than six months should consider seeking professional help such as that offered by psychotherapists.

Professional treatment helps more than 80% of all depressed patients, often within a few weeks.

The two primary therapies for depression are psychotherapy and antidepressant medication. In a study of 240 depressed patients, the National Institute of Mental Health found that both strategies are effective. The patients receiving antidepressants felt better faster, but those in psychotherapy did just as well within three months. By the end of the 16-week test period, more than half the patients in both forms of therapy no longer had serious symptoms of depression. The study also found that the combination of antidepressant drugs and psychotherapy was better than either therapy alone.

Certain approaches work better for different types of depression. Antidepressant drugs are uniquely effective in depressions that seem to be biological, such as manic depression. Psychotherapy alone is a treatment of choice for individuals who have not developed many "biological" symptoms, such as weight loss and sleep problems.

PSYCHOTHERAPY

The most widely used forms of therapy—often called "talking therapies"—are short-term, structured treatments, generally ranging from 12 to 20 sessions over a period of 12 to 16 weeks. Psychotherapy may take a number of different forms.

Cognitive therapy teaches patients to identify and change the way they think, and improve overly pessimistic views of themselves and the world. For instance, a depressed teenager may feel rejected when her friend is late for their scheduled lunch. "No one likes to be with me," she may conclude. In this situation, the therapist may point out the girl's negative thinking, noting that her friend had a legitimate excuse, apologized profusely, and made plans to go shopping with her the next weekend.

Interpersonal therapy focuses on current relationships and strategies for improving them. Its goal is to help patients develop more successful ways of relating to other people. One 18 year old became depressed because his relationships with girls never lasted. His therapist helped him identify a common problem in his relationships—his inability to express his feelings—and then helped him develop better communication skills.

Other approaches include behavioral treatment, which emphasizes self-monitoring to make sure patients recognize and reward their own actions. Another is family therapy, which provides a setting in which relatives can become more aware of each other's feelings and can see the impact of their own behavior on other family members.

MEDICATIONS

Antidepressant drugs correct the imbalance of brain chemicals typical in depression, usually within a few weeks. Therapists generally prescribe drugs for patients who (1) are severely depressed; (2) have physical symptoms, such as loss of appetite and weight, sleep disturbances, and fatigue; (3) have a family history of depression; (4) report cycles of mood or symptoms at specific times of the day, month, or year; (5) do not respond to psychological approaches.

The two types of medications used for unipolar depression—tricyclic antidepressants and monoamine oxidase (MAO) inhibitors—increase the supplies of the neurotransmitters norepinephrine and serotonin in the brain. Tricyclic antidepressants—so named because they have a three-ring chemical structure—have been a popular treatment for depression since the late 1950s. These drugs achieve their effects by increasing either the amount or the activity of dopamine and norepinephrine, which are two neurotransmitters, in the brain. Some tricyclic antidepressants, such as amitryptiline (Elavil) and doxepin (Sinequan) are sedatives; that is, they relieve agitation and anxiety. Imipramine (Tofranil) and desipramine (Norpramin) are not sedating, and can help people who suffer from lack of energy. Tricyclic antidepressants may take four to six weeks to produce significant improvement. They can cause various side effects, including shakiness, dry mouth, light-headedness, blurred vision, constipation, clumsiness, drowsiness, and weight gain. These are not considered serious. However, sometimes the patient suffers an abnormal heartbeat.

Once they recover from an episode of depression, most patients continue to take medication for 4 to 12 months. The use of tri-

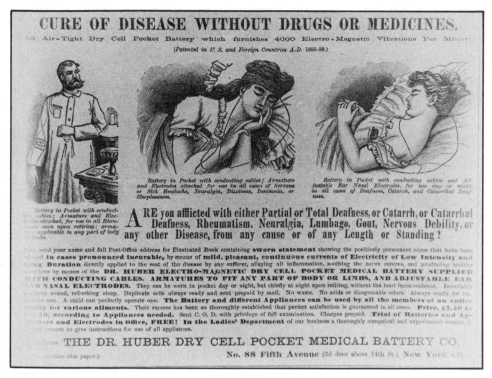

Electroconvulsive shock therapy, used in conjunction with antidepressants, has proved to be an effective treatment for depression.

cyclic antidepressants in adolescents has not yet been extensively studied in scientific experiments.

According to child psychiatrists Linda Gourash and Joaquim Puig-Antich, of the University of Pittsburgh, many doctors dispense only a one-week supply of medication because an overdose—deliberate or accidental—can cause seizures and serious heart problems.

Small-quantity prescriptions have another advantage, observes psychiatrist Domeena Renshaw of Loyola University: They "help ensure that the family soon returns to the physician for follow-up, thereby reducing the risk of suicide." The medication should be locked up and dispensed only by the parent to prevent that danger as well as the risk of accidental overdose by the child or his or her siblings.

MAO inhibitors are used primarily when patients do not improve while using tricyclic antidepressants or suffer from "atypical depression," which is characterized by anxiety, weight gain, sensitivity to rejection, self-pity, cravings for sweets and other carbohydrates, fatigue, and increased sleep. Side effects that occur more frequently include insomnia, daytime drowsiness, dry mouth, dizziness, and impotence.

MAO inhibitors have another potential drawback. They boost levels of tyramine, a natural chemical in the body, and high levels of tyramine can increase blood pressure. Thus, MAO inhibitors can indirectly cause high blood pressure, which, in some cases, can be life threatening. Because of this risk, MAO inhibitors are used less often than the tricyclics.

Lithium is a salt used to prevent or treat manic episodes in patients with manic, or bipolar, depression. After recovering from a manic episode, patients continue on a maintenance dose (low dose meant to prevent a recurrence) for at least a year. Patients with recurrent or severe mania may continue on lithium indefinitely. Use of this drug has reduced what was once a high suicide rate in victims of the disease.

The use of lithium by adolescents has not been thoroughly evaluated by researchers. Side effects are usually minor: tremors, thirst, dry mouth, frequent urination. Levels in the blood must be monitored because too-high amounts can cause serious side effects.

OTHER TREATMENTS

Some forms of depression respond to treatments that do not involve medications. For example, patients with winter seasonal affective disorder improve if they spend two hours a day throughout the winter months in front of a special fluorescent light that mimics natural sunlight. Initiating this treatment, which is called light therapy, in the fall can often prevent winter depression.

Usually the patient's mood lifts within three to five days and he or she remains free of depressive symptoms as long as light therapy is continued until the onset of spring. Some patients have developed transient headaches while using the lights; a few become overly agitated (an effect that can be prevented by cutting down on the duration of light exposure).

Electroconvulsive shock therapy is another option for those with major depression. ECT—the administration of a controlled electrical current through electrodes attached to the head—can jolt patients out of severe, psychotic, or life-threatening depression. About 70% to 80% of all patients who fail to respond to antidepressant medications improve after ECT. Because relapses can occur, patients take antidepressant drugs as well.

Recent improvements have reduced memory problems and other traumas once considered side effects of ECT. In ECT, patients are given an anesthetic and a muscle relaxant. Brief pulses of electricity are then passed through the brain from one electrode placed on the head to another, creating a seizure that lasts about a minute. Treatment generally consists of 6 to 12 ECT sessions, each 2 or 3 days apart. There is no evidence that properly administered ECT causes brain damage or permanent memory loss.

The best treatment for moderate depression is often a relaxing afternoon with friends or loved ones.

HOW FAMILY AND FRIENDS CAN HELP

Depressed individuals may not be capable of reaching out to others for help. But they need support from loved ones. If someone you know is depressed, you can help by treating that person as normally as possible and keeping him or her busy and active.

If your friend refuses your invitations, be gently assertive. Rather than taking no for an answer, show up at the door with your picnic basket in hand and head outdoors with your friend on a sunny day. Pick him or her up on your way to the mall or a movie.

Depressed people often feel guilty about feeling so bad. Try not to compound those feelings by blaming your friend for being down. Be patient. And keep in mind that what you say to your friend or what you do with him or her is less important than the simple fact that you show you care.

•　　　•　　　•　　　•

APPENDIX:
FOR MORE INFORMATION

The following national organizations can provide information about depression and therapy.

American Mental Health
   Foundation
2 East 86th Street
New York, NY 10028
(212) 737-9027

National Depressive and Manic
   Depressive Association
Box 3395
Chicago, IL 60654
(312) 993-0066

National Institute of Mental Health
Alcohol, Drug Abuse and Mental
   Health Administration
5600 Fishers Lane
Rockville, MD 20857

DEPRESSION TREATMENT CLINICS

The following is a list of local depression treatment centers and specialists around the country.

ALABAMA

University of Alabama School of
   Medicine
University Station
Birmingham, AL 35294
(205) 934-2011

ARIZONA

Southern Arizona Mental Health
   Center
1930 East Sixth Avenue
Tucson, AZ 85719
(602) 628-5221

ARKANSAS

University of Arkansas for Medical
　　Sciences
4301 West Markham
Suite 506
Little Rock, AR 72205
(501) 661-5266

CALIFORNIA

Langley Porter Neuropsychiatric
　　Institute
401 Parnassus Avenue
San Francisco, CA 94143
(415) 476-7478

University of California at Los
　　Angeles
Affective Disorders Clinic
760 Westwood Plaza—Box 18
Los Angeles, CA 90024
(213) 825-0764, -0271, or -0491

COLORADO

University of Colorado Medical
　　Center
4200 East Ninth Avenue
Denver, CO 80220
(303) 394-8403

CONNECTICUT

University School of Medicine
Depression Research Unit
350 Congress Avenue
New Haven, CT 06519
(203) 785-5550

FLORIDA

University of Miami Medical Center
Box 016960
Miami, FL 33101
(305) 674-2194

GEORGIA

Emory University School of Medicine
Emory Outpatient Clinic
1365 Clifton Road NW
Atlanta, GA 30322
(404) 321-0111

HAWAII

University of Hawaii
Department of Psychiatry
1356 Lusitana Street
Honolulu, HI 96813
(808) 548-3420

ILLINOIS

Rush Medical College
1720 West Polk Street
Chicago, IL 60612
(312) 942-5372

IOWA

University of Iowa
Department of Psychiatry
500 Newton Road
Iowa City, IA 52242
(319) 353-3719

KANSAS

University of Kansas School of
　　Medicine
Department of Psychiatry
Kansas City, KS 67214
(913) 261-2647

KENTUCKY

University of Kentucky
Department of Psychiatry
Lexington, KY 40536
(606) 233-6005

LOUISIANA

Tulane Medical Center
Department of Psychiatry
1415 Tulane Avenue
New Orleans, LA 70112
(504) 588-5236

MARYLAND

National Institute of Mental Health
9000 Rockville Pike
Building 10, Room 4S-239
Bethesda, MD 20892
(301) 496-5755 or -2141

MASSACHUSETTS

Massachusetts Mental Health
  Center
74 Fenwood Road
Boston, MA 02115
(617) 731-2921

MICHIGAN

Department of Psychiatry
University Hospital
7500 East Medical Center Drive
Ann Arbor, MI 48109
(313) 763-9629

MINNESOTA

University of Minnesota Medical
  School
Minneapolis, MN 55455
(612) 373-8869

MISSISSIPPI

University of Mississippi
School of Medicine
Department of Psychiatry and
  Human Behavior
2500 North State Street
Jackson, MS 39216
(314) 362-2474

NEBRASKA

University of Nebraska
Nebraska Psychiatric
  Institute
602 South 45th Street
Omaha, NE 68106
(402) 572-2955

NEVADA

University of Nevada School of
  Medicine
Department of Psychiatry and
  Behavioral Sciences
Reno, NV 89557
(702) 784-4917

NEW HAMPSHIRE

Dartmouth-Hitchcock Medical
  Center
Community Mental Health Center
Hanover, NH 03755
(603) 646-5000, ext. 5855

NEW JERSEY

Fair Oaks Hospital
19 Prospect Street
Summit, NJ 07901
(201) 522-7000

NEW MEXICO

University of New Mexico School of
  Medicine
Department of Psychiatry
2400 Tucker NE
Albuquerque, NM 87131
(505) 277-2223

NEW YORK

New York University Medical
  Center
560 First Avenue
New York, NY 10016
(212) 240-5707

University of Rochester
Department of Psychiatry
Affective Disorders Clinic
300 Crittenden Boulevard
Rochester, NY 14642
(716) 275-7818

NORTH CAROLINA

University of North Carolina
School of Medicine
Division of Health Affairs
Chapel Hill, NC 27514
(919) 966-1480

NORTH DAKOTA

University of North Dakota
Medical Education Center
1919 North Elm
Fargo, ND 58102
(701) 293-4113

DEPRESSION

OHIO

Central Psychiatric Clinic
3259 Elland Avenue
Mail Location 539
Cincinnati, OH 45267
(513) 872-5856

OKLAHOMA

University of Oklahoma
Health Sciences Center and
    Behavioral Sciences
Department of Psychiatry
P.O. Box 26901
Oklahoma City, OK 73190
(405) 271-5251

OREGON

Portland Division V.A.
3710 S. West U.S. Veterans
    Hospital Road
P.O. Box 1034
Portland, OR 97207
(503) 222-9221

PENNSYLVANIA

Medical College of Pennsylvania at
    Eastern Pennsylvania
Psychiatric Institute
3200 Henry Avenue
Philadelphia, PA 19129
(215) 597-7168 or -7169

RHODE ISLAND

V.A. Hospital of Providence
Providence, RI 02908
(401) 273-7100

SOUTH CAROLINA

Medical University of South
    Carolina
Psychiatric Outpatient Department
171 Ashley Avenue
Charleston, SC 29425
(803) 792-4037

TENNESSEE

Vanderbilt University
Department of Psychiatry
Nashville, TN 37232
(615) 322-4927

TEXAS

University of Texas, Medical
    Branch
Department of Psychiatry and
    Behavioral Science
1200 Graves Building
Galveston, TX 77550
(409) 761-3901

UTAH

University of Utah
College of Medicine
Department of Psychiatry
50 North Medical Drive
Salt Lake City, UT 84132
(801) 581-4888

VIRGINIA

Eastern Virginia Medical School
    Department of Psychiatry and
    Behavioral Sciences
P.O. Box 1980
Norfolk, VA 23501
(804) 446-5888

WASHINGTON

Harbor View Medical Center
Psychiatry Department
2H Harbor View Hall
325 Ninth Avenue
Seattle, WA 98104
(206) 223-3404

SUICIDE PREVENTION CENTERS

The following list offers a sampling of suicide prevention centers that are available 24 hours a day and are certified by the American Association of Suicidology. A complete directory of suicide prevention and crisis intervention centers around the country can be obtained by writing to the Association, at 2459 South Ash, Denver, CO, 80222.

ALABAMA

Crisis Center of Jefferson County
3600 Eighth Avenue South
Birmingham, AL 35222
Crisis Phone: (205) 323-7777
Business Phone: (205) 323-7782

ALASKA

Fairbanks Crisis Clinic Foundation
P.O. Box 832
Fairbanks, AK 99707
Crisis Phone: (907) 452-4403
Business Phone: (907) 479-0166

CALIFORNIA

Los Angeles Suicide Prevention
  Center
1041 South Menlo
Los Angeles, CA 90006
Crisis Phone: (213) 381-5111
Business Phone: (213) 386-5111

COLORADO

Pueblo Suicide Prevention, Inc.
229 Colorado Avenue
Pueblo, CO 81004
Crisis Phone: (303) 544-1133
Business Phone: (303) 545-2477

CONNECTICUT

The Wheeler Clinic, Inc.
Emergency Services
91 Northwest Drive
Plainville, CT 06062
Crisis Phone 1: (203) 747-3434
Crisis Phone 2: (203) 524-1182
Business Phone: (203) 747-6801

FLORIDA

Alucha County Crisis Center
730 North Waldo Road, Suite #100
Gainesville, FL 32601
Crisis Phone 1: (904) 376-4444
Crisis Phone 2: (904) 376-4445
Business Phone: (904) 372-3659

ILLINOIS

Call For Help
Suicide & Crisis Intervention
  Service
500 Wilshire Drive
Belleville, IL 62223
Crisis Phone: (618) 397-0963
Business Phone: (618) 397-0968

KENTUCKY

Seven Counties Services
Crisis & Information Center
600 South Preston Street
Louisville, KY 40202
Crisis Phone: (502) 589-4313
Business Phone: (502) 583-3951,
  ext. 284

LOUISIANA

Baton Rouge Crisis Intervention
  Center
P.O. Box 80738
Baton Rouge, LA 70898
Crisis Phone: (504) 924-3900
Business Phone: (504) 924-1595

MARYLAND

Montgomery County Hotline
10920 Connecticut Avenue
Kensington, MD 20795
Crisis Phone: (301) 949-6603
Business Phone: (301) 949-1255

DEPRESSION

MASSACHUSETTS

The Samaritans
500 Commonwealth Avenue
Boston, MA 02215
Crisis Phone: (617) 247-0220
Business Phone: (617) 536-2460

MICHIGAN

Suicide Prevention Center/Detroit
220 Bagley, Suite 626
Detroit, MI 48226
Crisis Phone: (313) 224-7000
Business Phone: (313) 963-7890

MINNESOTA

Crisis Intervention Center
Hennepin County Medical Center
701 Park Avenue South
Minneapolis, MN 55415
Crisis Phone: (612) 347-3161
Suicide Hotline: (612) 347-2222
Crisis Home Program:
(612) 347-3170
Sexual Assault Service:
(612) 347-5838
Business Phone: (612) 347-3100

MISSOURI

Life Crisis Services, Inc.
1423 South Big Bend Boulevard
St. Louis, MO 63117
Crisis Phone: (314) 647-4357
Business Phone: (314) 647-3100

NEW HAMPSHIRE

Center for Life Management
Salem Professional Park
44 Stiles Road
Salem, NH 03079
Crisis Phone: (606) 432-2253
Business Phone: (606) 893-3548

NEW YORK

Suicide Prevention & Crisis Service
P.O. Box 312
Ithaca, NY 14850
Crisis Phone: (607) 272-1616
Business Phone: (607) 272-1505

NORTH CAROLINA

Suicide & Crisis Service/Alamance
   County
P.O. Box 2573
Burlington, NC 27215
Crisis Phone: (919) 227-6220
Business Phone: (919) 228-1720

OHIO

Support, Inc.
1361 West Market Street
Akron, OH 44313
Crisis Phone: (216) 434-9114
Business Phone: (216) 864-7743

PENNSYLVANIA

Contact Pittsburgh, Inc.
P.O. Box 30
Glenshaw, PA 15116
Crisis Phone: (412) 782-4023
Business Phone: (412) 487-7712

TENNESSEE

Crisis Intervention Center, Inc.
P.O. Box 120934
Nashville, TN 37212
Crisis Phone: (615) 244-7444
Business Phone: (615) 928-3359

TEXAS

Suicide & Crisis Center
2808 Swiss Avenue
Dallas, TX 75204
Crisis Phone: (214) 828-1000
Business Phone: (214) 824-7020

VIRGINIA

Northern Virginia Hotline
P.O. Box 187
Arlington, VA 22210
Crisis Phone: (703) 527-4077
Business Phone: (703) 522-4460

WASHINGTON

Crisis Clinic
1530 Eastlake East
Seattle, WA 98102
Crisis Phone: (206) 447-3222
Business Phone: (206) 447-3210

The following associations are certified suicide prevention centers located in Canada; crisis phones operate 24 hours a day, 7 days a week. Each center can provide the address and phone number of local centers.

ALBERTA

Aid Service of Edmonton
#203-10711 107th Avenue
Edmonton, Alberta T5H OW6
Crisis Phone: (403) 426-4252
Business Phone: (403) 426-3242

Distress Centre/Drug Centre
112-11 Avenue SE 201 Regency Bld
Calgary, Alberta T2G OX5
Crisis Phone: (403)-266-1605
Teen Line: (403) 266-1608
Business Phone: (403) 266-1601

BRITISH COLUMBIA

Crisis Intervention and Prevention
  Centre
1946 West Broadway
Vancouver, British Columbia
V6J 1Z2
Business Phone: (604) 733-1171

Nanaimo Association for
  Intervention and Development
P.O. Box 1118
Nanaimo, British Columbia
V9R 6E7
Crisis Phones: (604) 754-4447 and
  -4448
Business Phone: (604) 753-2495

MANITOBA

Health Sciences Centre
59 Pearl Street
Winnipeg, Manitoba R3E 3L7

ONTARIO

Department of Psychiatry
Toronto East General Hospital
825 Coxwell Avenue
Toronto, Ontario M4C 3E7
Business Phone: (416) 461-0311

St. Joseph's Hospital
l50 Charlton Avenue East
Hamilton, Ontario L8N 4A6
Business Phone: (416) 522-4941

QUEBEC

Centre De Prevention Du Suicide,
  Inc.
141 Rue St. Jean
Quebec G1R 1N4
Crisis Phone: (418) 525-4588
Business Phone: (418) 525-4628

Suicide-Action Montreal, Inc.
4651 Rue St. Denis
Montreal, Quebec H2J 2L5
Crisis Phone: (514) 522-5777
Business Phone: (514) 842-9287

FURTHER READING

American Health Research Institute. *Depression: Medical Subject Analysis and Research Directory with Bibliography*. J. C. Bartone, ed. Washington, DC: ABBE Publishers Association of Washington, DC, 1982.

Andersen, N. C. *The Broken Brain: The Biological Revolution in Psychiatry*. New York: Harper & Row, 1984.

Beckham, Ernest Edward, and William R. Lever, eds. *Handbook of Depression: Treatment, Assessment, and Research*. Homewood, IL: Dorsey Press, 1985.

Bohn, J., and J. W. Jefferson. *Lithium and Manic Depression*. 4th revision. Madison, Wisconsin: Lithium Information Center, University of Wisconsin, 1987.

Cherry, Lawrence. "The Good News About Depression." *New York Times Magazine*, June 2, 1986.

Cohn, Jeffrey, and Edward Tronick. "Three Month Old Infant's Reaction to Simulated Maternal Depression." *Child Development*. February 1983, 54:1(185–93).

Costello, Charles Gerard. *Anxiety and Depression: The Adaptive Emotions*. Montreal: McGill-Queen's University Press, 1976.

Coyne, James C., ed. *Essential Papers on Depression*. New York: New York University Press, 1986, 1985.

Fieve, Ronald, M.D. *Moodswing: The Third Revolution in Psychiatry*. New York: Bantam, 1976.

Gaylin, Willard, ed. *Psychodynamic Understanding of Depression: The Meaning of Despair*. New York: J. Aronson, 1983.

Good, Byron, and Arthur Kleinman, eds. *Culture and Depression: Studies in the Anthropology and Cross-Cultural Psychiatry of Affect and Disorder*. Berkeley: University of California Press, 1985.

Greist, John H., M.D., and James W. Jefferson, M.D. *Depression and Its Treatment*. New York: American Psychiatrist/Warner Books, 1984.

Hershman, D. Jaklow, and Julian Lieb, M.D. *The Key to Genius: Manic-Depression and the Creative Life*. New York: Prometheus, 1988.

Izard, Carrol E., Peter B. Read, and Michael Rutter. *Depression in Young People: Development and Clinical Perspectives*. New York: Gilford Press, 1986.

Jackson, Stanley W. *Melancholia and Depression: From Hippocratic Times to the Present*. New Haven: Yale University Press, 1986.

Klein, Donald F., M.D., and Paul W. Wender, M.D. *Do You Have a Depressive Illness?* New York: New American Library Books, 1988.

————. *Mind, Mood, and Medicine*. New York: Farrar, Straus & Giroux, 1981.

Klerman, Gerald L., ed. *Suicide and Depression Among Adolescents and Young Adults*. Washington, DC: American Psychiatric Press, 1986.

Kline, N. S. *From Sad to Glad*. New York: Ballantine, 1981.

Levitt, Eugene E. *Depression: Concepts, Controversies, and Some New Facts*. New York: Springer Publications, 1975.

Mahendra, Bala. *Depression: The Disorder and Its Associations*. Boston: MTP Press, 1987.

Maser, Jack, ed. *Depression and Expressive Behavior*. Hillsdale, NJ: L. Erlbaum Associates, 1987.

Mendelson, Myer. *Psychoanalytic Concepts of Depression*. 2nd ed. Flushing, NY: Spectrum Publications, distributed by Halstead Press, NY, 1974.

Papolos, Demitri, M.D., and Janice Papolos. *Overcoming Depression*. New York: Harper & Row, 1987.

Romanis, Robert. *Depression*. Boston: Faber and Faber, 1987.

Schmeck, Harold M., Jr. "Depression: Studies Bring New Drugs." *New York Times*, February 6, 1988.

Wetzel, Janice Wood. *Clinical Handbook of Depression*. New York: Gardner Press, 1984.

GLOSSARY

anorexia nervosa an eating disorder characterized by an obsession with thinness and by loss of appetite; results in extreme weight loss

antidepressant a medication that lessens the effects of depression; such a drug is thought to do so by correcting the imbalance of brain chemicals

bipolar disorder a mood disorder characterized by episodes of depression and of mania; also referred to as manic depression

chromosome rodlike structure within the cell that carries genetic information

cognitive therapy a treatment for depression that emphasizes correction of negative or irrational attitudes or thoughts

cyclothymia a disorder in which a person experiences numerous episodes of depression and hypomania but whose symptoms do not recur often enough or with enough severity to classify as characteristic of manic depression

delusion false belief firmly held despite obvious proof to the contrary

depression as a mood, feelings of sadness, despair, and discouragement; as a disorder, a syndrome of associated symptoms, including decreased pleasure, slowed thinking, sadness, hopelessness, guilt, and disrupted sleeping and eating patterns

dysthymia morbid, long-term anxiety or sadness accompanied by obsession

ECT electroconvulsive treatment; also called electroshock treatment; method of treating certain types of psychosis by using electric current to induce convulsive seizures

euphoria an exaggerated feeling of well-being

genetic related to genes or inherited characteristics

guilt emotion resulting from doing what is perceived as wrong

hyperactivity a disorder characterized by excessive bodily activity

hypersomnia a disorder characterized by excessive sleep

hypomania a disorder of mood characterized by unrealistic optimism, rapid speech or activity, and decreased need for sleep

interpersonal therapy a form of psychotherapy that focuses on achieving good relationships with others

learned helplessness a depression-causing state in which an unavoidable setback, such as an accident or illness, makes a person feel helpless; the condition may spread to other situations until he or she feels utterly overwhelmed

learning disability any one of a wide range of disabilities, most of which impair reading skills and, sometimes, writing skills; can also cause trouble listening, speaking, reasoning, or doing math; some learning-disabled people also have psychological problems or are slow to develop motor skills, and many have more than one disability

major depression an episode of depression so severe that it impairs normal functioning

mania a psychological state characterized by excitement, euphoria, rapid speech, flight of ideas, high energy, distractibility, irritability, and impaired judgment

manic depression a mood disorder characterized by episodes of depression and of mania

melancholia ancient Greek term for depression

melatonin a sleep-inducing hormone produced by the brain in the dark hours and linked to seasonal affective disorder

mood a pervasive, sustained emotion that colors the way a person perceives the world

mood disorder psychiatric term used for unipolar and bipolar depression

neurotransmitter a chemical released by neurons that transmits nerve impulses across a synapse

norepinephrine a neurotransmitter, an imbalance of which marks some forms of depression

PMS premenstrual syndrome; a physical syndrome with psychological side effects that include depression

psychomotor referring to physical behavior associated with mental activity

psychosis a major mental disorder that severely impairs a person's ability to think and communicate

psychotherapy treatment of psychological problems through mental rather than physical activity, especially by talking with a trained professional

psychotic depression depression in which a person develops psychotic symptoms and loses touch with reality

SAD seasonal affective disorder; form of depression related to seasonal variations in light and temperature

serotonin a neurotransmitter, an imbalance of which marks some forms of depression

suicide self-inflicted death; sometimes a consequence of severe depression

suppressed anger depression-causing state in which an individual, unable to express the normal anger that develops in daily living, may turn that anger inward on him or herself

unipolar depression mood disorder characterized by one or more episodes of depression

unresolved grief psychological state caused by not mourning or coming to terms with a loss; can breed feelings of sadness and anger and may eventually produce a deep-rooted sense of unhappiness, low self-esteem, hopelessness, and extreme sensitivity to rejection

INDEX

Abraham, Karl, 36
Adrenal gland, 53
Albert Einstein College of Medicine, 67
Alexander of Tralles, 26
American Journal of Psychiatry, 56, 60
American Journal of Public Health, 68
American Psychiatric Association (APA), 14, 15, 19, 22, 71
American Psychiatric Press Review of Psychiatry, 16, 48, 63, 69
American Psychiatric Press Textbook of Psychiatry, 38
Amitriptyline (Elavil), 80
Anatomy of Melancholy, The (Burton), 27
Anorexia nervosa, 40
Antidepressant medications, 16, 36, 58, 79, 80–82, 83
  tricyclic, 80–81
Aretaeus, 26
Aristotle, 24, 25
Axon, 66

Bipolar depression. *See* Manic depression
Birth control pills, 52
  link to depression, 52
Bloodletting, 24, 31
  as treatment for depression, 24, 31
Brain, 53
  hypothalamic region, 53
Bucknill, John Charles, 32
Burton, Robert, 27

Caffeine, 53
  link to depression, 53
Celsus, Aulus Cornelius, 24
Child abuse, 67
Child Development, 56
Chromosomes, 48
Clinical depression, 51
Clinical Psychology (Dubovsky), 49
Cohn, Jeffrey, 56
Columbia University, 48, 67
Cortisol, 53
Cullen, William, 30
Cyclomania, 45
  symptoms of, 45

Dendrite, 66
Depression
  adolescent, 14, 18, 19, 55, 58–60
    factors contributing to, 60–62
  adult, 18
  and alcohol use, 19, 38, 54
  and anxiety, 19
  biologically based, 16
  cause of, 23, 35–36, 47–54
    early life experiences, 48
    environment, 47, 54
    family, 48
    genetic, 44, 47, 48
    relationships, 48
    social, 47
    stress, 47
    trauma, 47
  and children, 14, 18, 55, 56–58
  chronic, 15
  clinical, 20, 22, 36, 51
  cyclomania, 45

PICTURE CREDITS

The Bettman Archive: pp. 25, 26, 29, 30, 31, 33, 34, 35, 41; Laimute E. Druskis/Taurus Photos: pp. 18, 19, 57, 61; Spencer Grant/Taurus Photos: p. 63; Eric Kroll/Taurus Photos: p. 39; Library of Congress: pp. 13, 14; National Institute of Mental Health/Courtesy of Nancy Low and Associates, Inc.: cover; National Library of Medicine: pp. 15, 23, 81; Karen R. Preuss/ Taurus Photos: p. 77; Martin M. Rotker/Taurus Photos: p. 49; Jean-Marie Simon/Taurus Photos: p. 59; Frank Siteman/Taurus Photos: pp. 17, 55, 58, 76; Wide World: pp. 21, 37, 43, 47, 65, 68, 72, 75, 78; Shirley Zeiberg/Taurus Photos: pp. 50, 51, 53, 83; Original illustrations by Gary Tong: p. 52

Dianne Hales is the author or coauthor of 10 books, including *The Family* and *Pregnancy and Birth* in Chelsea House's ENCYCLOPEDIA OF HEALTH, *An Invitation to Health: Your Personal Responsibility, The U.S. Army Total Fitness Program, The Complete Book of Sleep,* and *New Hope for Problem Pregnancies.* She is a contributing editor of *American Health* magazine and a frequent contributor to other magazines, including *McCall's, Redbook,* and *Parade.* Ms. Hales has also written for the *Washington Post,* the *New York Times, American Medical News, Medical World News,* and *Psychiatric News.*

Solomon H. Snyder, M.D., is Distinguished Service Professor of Neuroscience, Pharmacology, and Psychiatry and director of the Department of Neuroscience at the Johns Hopkins University School of Medicine. He has served as president of the Society for Neuroscience and in 1978 received the Albert Lasker Award in Medical Research for his discovery of opiate receptors in the brain. Dr. Snyder is a member of the National Academy of Sciences and a Fellow of the American Academy of Arts and Sciences. He is the author of *Drugs and the Brain, Uses of Marijuana, Madness and the Brain, The Troubled Mind,* and *Biological Aspects of Mental Disorder.* He is also the general editor of Chelsea House's ENCYCLOPEDIA OF PSYCHOACTIVE DRUGS.

C. Everett Koop, M.D., Sc.D., is Surgeon General, Deputy Assistant Secretary for Health, and Director of the Office of International Health of the U.S. Public Health Service. A pediatric surgeon with an international reputation, he was previously surgeon-in-chief of Children's Hospital of Philadelphia and professor of pediatric surgery and pediatrics at the University of Pennsylvania. Dr. Koop is the author of more than 175 articles and books on the practice of medicine. He has served as surgery editor of the *Journal of Clinical Pediatrics* and editor-in-chief of the *Journal of Pediatric Surgery.* Dr. Koop has received nine honorary degrees and numerous other awards, including the Denis Brown Gold Medal of the British Association of Paediatric Surgeons, the William E. Ladd Gold Medal of the American Academy of Pediatrics, and the Copernicus Medal of the Surgical Society of Poland. He is a Chevalier of the French Legion of Honor and a member of the Royal College of Surgeons, London.